ELEPHANT
GRASS

ELEPHANT GRASS

JOHN COWELL

JOHN BLAKE

Published by John Blake Publishing Ltd,
3 Bramber Court, 2 Bramber Road,
London W14 9PB, England

www.johnblakepublishing.co.uk

First published in paperback in 2009

ISBN: 978-1-84454-711-1

British Library Cataloguing-in-Publication Data:

A catalogue record for this book is available from the British Library.

Design by www.envydesign.co.uk

Printed in the UK by CPI William Clowes Ltd, Beccles, NR34 7TL

1 3 5 7 9 10 8 6 4 2

Papers used by John Blake Publishing are natural, recyclable products made from
wood grown in sustainable forests. The manufacturing processes conform to the
environmental regulations of the country of origin.

Every attempt has been made to contact the relevant copyright-holders, but some
were unobtainable. We would be grateful if the appropriate people could contact us.

I dedicate this book to my two sons and all my grandchildren.

ACKNOWLEDGEMENTS

I would like to thank all my friends and family who encouraged me to write these memoirs about my time in Africa during my National Service days.

My gratitude is expressed personally to my friend Agnes Kershaw, my son Craig, my cousin Michael Walsh and Madeleine Fish, all of whom painstakingly proof-read my book. Also, to Vicky McGeown, of John Blake Publishing, who came up with some wonderful suggestions.

Many thanks to my friends, Martin Grogan and Howard Fanshaw from Burnley, Duggie Smith from Liverpool, Brian Holdsworth from Leeds, Robert MacNaughton from Halesowen and Alan Parkinson from Barrow in Furness, who were stationed alongside me in the Cameroons and supplied invaluable photographs of our little adventure in the tropical jungle country. My special thanks are due to Alan Parkinson for his detailed personal account while out on patrol, as described in chapter six.

ELEPHANT GRASS

Further thanks go to Craig for designing the front cover and for setting up a website for my book. I must also say thank you to my other son John and my ex-wife Edna for all their encouragement when my spirit was flagging.

Finally I thank you, the readers, for giving me the confidence to write another story.

viii

CONTENTS

INTRODUCTION

I never expected to be writing yet another book but thanks to you, dear readers, I've got the confidence to do so. My first book, *The Broken Biscuit*, was the story of my mother's life – how she raised a large family during the Second World War in the era of clogs and shawls. Its success was far beyond my expectations; I received many letters from all over the UK, Spain, America and Australia, and each one asked me to write another story. What gave me the most satisfaction was that I'd brought a little pleasure into other people's lives. I would like to take this opportunity to thank all you kind people for your wonderful, inspiring letters.

My second book, *Cracks in the Ceiling*, ended with me marching off to the Cameroons in West Africa. The reason I finished my tale at that point was because from then on my life changed completely. I was leaving all the cotton mills, factory chimneys, cobbled streets and poverty of post-war Britain behind me, but for the next eight months I was to work alongside even more impoverished people living in little mud huts, struggling every day for a bite to eat. *Elephant Grass* is the story of my experiences in the British Cameroons during my National Service days.

Mandatory call-up to serve one's country was introduced during the Second World War, but was later extended into peacetime National Service. Every man, on reaching the age of 18, was called upon to serve two years in Her Majesty's Forces. The only men exempt from the scheme were coal miners, farmers or those in other industries on which the country depended.

Unlike regular soldiers, lads called up under the National Service system had no option but to go into whatever regiment they were allocated to. They were put through an arduous training regime and then placed on emergency standby, to be posted to a troubled state anywhere in the world. In my case I was placed into the Royal Army Medical Corps and sent to the Cameroons, where I was attached to a fine, upstanding regiment – The King's Own Borderers.

The British Cameroons was a slim strip of territory between two much bigger neighbours: Nigeria (from which it was ruled) and the French Cameroons. The terrain on the western border is mountainous from Lake Chad in the north to Mount Cameroon in the south. The north is tall grasslands, whereas the south is tropical lowlands. But the central region is different again, being covered in thick, tropical jungle. Cameroon was a very poor Third World country; most of the people were farmers but some were herders of cattle. Yet despite terrible poverty these people were friendly, loving and generous to a fault… I'll let you judge for yourself.

John Cowell

CHAPTER ONE

ARMY DISCIPLINE

It was late August 1960 and the sun was shining brightly as I made my way down Albion Street heading for the railway station. I felt rather sad as I had just said my goodbyes to my family and could still picture my mum stood at the garden gate, waving me off, with tears in her eyes.

'Look after yourself, our John, and make sure you eat well,' she said affectionately. 'And don't take any silly risks while you're out there in Africa.'

'Don't worry, mam,' I replied, giving her a hug to reassure her. 'I'll try my best to keep out of trouble.'

The reason for my mother's concern was because I was in the Army. Thirteen months earlier I had been called up to serve two years' National Service in Her Majesty's Forces and now I, along with the other troops, was being shipped abroad to West Africa on active service.

As I walked down the terraced street I stopped at No. 14, the house that contained all my childhood memories. Prior to being called up into the forces it was the only house I'd ever lived in. It was now deserted as, like all the others on the block, it was due to be demolished.

As I stood there I got a strong compelling feeling to go in and take a last look around before it came under the hammer. I knew I would never get the opportunity to do so again. As I entered the living room with its bare stone-flagged floor and cast-iron fireplace, nostalgic memories raced through my head.

I could see myself sat on Mum's knee while she told me stories of her childhood days in the small Lancashire town of Bacup. My brothers and sisters were sat around listening intently. Sometimes tears would well up in their eyes with the sadness of it all and other times they would burst into fits of laughter. That's how it used to be at No. 14.

My eyes then gazed at the pot sink, which stood on cast-iron legs under a sliding sash-window. A flimsy, flea-ridden curtain billowed from the draught of a rotting windowsill. I then looked at the old gas lamp that hung from the ceiling, never to be lit again.

My mind drifted again and I could see Dad in one of his frivolous moods doing an Irish jig in front of the fire, his pants rolled up to his knees. He looked so funny as he danced on the old pegged rug, showing off his skinny knees – they looked like picking sticks. Mum used to say there was more meat on a ginny spinner's legs than Dad's.

I climbed the stairs and went into the girls' bedroom and glanced over the rooftops of the neighbouring houses, where I could see the town-hall clock in all its glory.

Then I walked into the front bedroom, where I'd slept with my two brothers. In the alcove nearest the window I noticed the pencil marks that my siblings had scribbled down over the years, indicating the progress of our growth. Beside them were excited comments added by whoever had grown the most at that time.

Finally I looked at the exact place where our bed had been; the place where I'd said my prayers every night, alongside my brothers, before going to sleep. At that I knelt down and said my last prayers in that humble little house and asked God to keep a vigilant watch over me and my comrades, and to take care of Mum and the rest of the family while I was away.

As I left the house, and walked down the steep cobbled street, a feeling of sadness enveloped me once again. On reaching the bottom of the street I took a last look back, took a long deep breath, and then marched briskly along Trafalgar and headed for Barracks railway station.

Thoughts of my childhood flashed through my mind once again as I sat on the train back to Plymouth, having just spent a few days on embarkation leave in my home town of Burnley. Despite the abject poverty, I could only remember the happy times growing up in 14 Albion Street with my three sisters and two brothers. We were poor, but there had always been love in abundance and I wouldn't have swapped it for anything. Suddenly my life had taken a dramatic turn and everything seemed topsy-turvy. During the past year Mum had moved out of our home of 20 years, set among the cotton mills and cobbled streets of Trafalgar, into a council house on the Rosehill Estate, I'd been called up into the forces and, saddest of all, my dad had died.

Now at 21 years of age, I was travelling back to camp in Plymouth, Devon, with the world at my feet. I was on my way to a foreign land with a feeling of eager anticipation, albeit tinged with some foreboding. My excitement stemmed from the fact that all my life I'd lived in the most congested part of an extremely busy cotton town, and for the first five years of my working life had toiled underground in the wet and dusty conditions of a coalmine. Now new horizons beckoned me.

Factory chimneys dominated the town's skyline, belching out thick dense smoke from umpteen weaving sheds, covering the cobbled streets and small cluttered houses in grime. The damp atmosphere of the town made it an ideal location for the cotton trade, as the humidity was good for weaving cloth. Most townsfolk lived in back-to-back terraced houses that had been built in the 1840s for the mill workers. The squalid conditions had taken their toll; many people suffered from arthritis, bronchitis, emphysema and other crippling diseases, so the prospect of going to a sunny climate thrilled me.

However, I was also anxious because, along with my mates, I was being shipped off to the British Cameroons in West Africa.

There had been a recent uprising in the Belgian Congo and the British and French Cameroons were seeking independence. Our mission was to keep the peace during a plebiscite, which was to determine whether the British Cameroons would join Nigeria or the French Cameroons. Guerilla activity was rife on the British and French border, but it was far worse within the French territory. I liked the idea of going abroad but I didn't fancy going to a war zone.

'Bloomin' 'eck,' I murmured to myself. 'I remember all those tales my grandad used to tell me about the First World War. The poor soul went away to that bloomin' war full of enthusiasm, but according to what he told me it was horrible!' I felt very deeply for my grandad, as he'd spent four long years living and sleeping in cold wet trenches on the Western Front, seeing many of his mates killed in action and many more die due to the atrocious conditions.

The 'diddly-dum, diddly-dum' sound of the train wheels on the tracks temporarily interrupted my thoughts, but it wasn't long before my mind started to wander again. It might not be as cold in Africa as it was for my grandad in France, but I still didn't fancy going into battle against anyone. A shudder ran down my spine as I imagined hundreds of African warriors charging at me, wielding long spears and machetes. At least I wasn't alone in my quandary, as I was to find out later.

Fourteen months earlier I had received official papers from the War Office in London, conscripting me into Her Majesty's Forces to serve two years' National Service. Against my will, the powers that be had placed me into the Royal Army Medical Corps

(RAMC). My title was now Private Cowell, number 23633183. I protested strongly, requesting to be put into another regiment, but to no avail. Nevertheless, things turned out all right. After a few months I settled down and actually enjoyed working as a nursing orderly in the Army hospitals.

On enlistment I'd reported to Queen Elizabeth Barracks in Crookham, Hampshire, where, along with more young men, I underwent 16 weeks of rigorous training. By the end of the course we were all well versed in First Aid and certain nursing duties. It was during this time that I made friends with Jimmy Mitchinson from Wigan, Brian Holdsworth from Leeds, Robert (better known as Rob) MacNaughton from Halesowen, Johnny Church from Liverpool and many others.

After completing the intensive training I was posted to Seaton Barracks in the Crownhill area of Plymouth, along with some of my new friends. It was at this new posting that I met Ernie Christie, a lad from my home town, and he was the fittest soldier on the camp. After a day's slogging he would think nothing of doing a ten-mile run just for the fun of it. During the summer months I used to join him, and we spent many hours on Dartmoor trying to break in some of the wild ponies; it was like being in a Wild West bucking bronco competition.

'C'mon, John,' he said one Saturday. 'Let's have a run over to Princetown where the prison is. You never know, we may see some of the prisoners.'

'I don't think so, Ernie,' I replied. 'There are a lot of life-timers in there and some are murderers.'

'Ah well, never mind – it'll still be interesting to see the prison.'

'Yeah, fair enough then. Let's go!'

So we did set off and to my surprise we actually saw some prisoners, doing menial gardening jobs away from the confines of the jail. We talked to one of them and he was only in his early thirties. He informed us that he'd already served 10 years and that now he was a trustee with only two more years to go. I didn't ask him what he was in for, but the thought crossed my mind that 12 years out of his young life was an awful waste.

On the way back to camp Ernie made it known that his thoughts on the matter were the same as mine. 'I'll tell you what, John, I wouldn't like to be locked up like them poor souls. I couldn't bear it. Just the thought of what they're missing out on makes me cringe. I can imagine them living in dismal surroundings, grey walls and limited perimeters. I'd die if I had to live in imprisonment like that for years on end. They put me in mind of young birds being trapped in a cruel cage.'

'I know what you mean, Ernie: they're missing out on all this open countryside and the wonders of nature.'

'Yeah, it makes me think about my own precious freedom and how I take the everyday things for granted. I love the touch of warm sunshine on my skin and to feel the wind blowing in my face. Just listen to the singing of those birds nesting over there in that magnificent tree – I'd hate to miss out on all this wonderful countryside. Yeah, this is the life for me.'

He certainly impressed me with his love of nature and his

outlook on life. He was a very clean-living man and didn't smoke or drink; he spent his time out in the open, taking in the fresh air at every opportunity.

'Come off it, Ernie!' I said, 'You're one person who definitely doesn't take things for granted. I don't know anyone who is more of a nature lover than you, and it's obvious why you're in prime condition.'

As we made our way back we came across a slow-flowing stream with a small waterfall, and a large expanse of water which had built up in a deep gully.

'How do you fancy a dip, John?' Ernie enthused, 'It'll be a great way to cool off!'

'I'm all for that, matey – let's go for it!'

The water was quite deep and a large rock on the bank made an ideal diving platform. We swam in the cool water and splashed about under the gentle cascade for a good two hours and then just lazed about sunbathing on the grassy embankment. The idyllic surroundings put Ernie into a nostalgic mood once again.

'Just listen to the sound of the waterfall, John! It reminds me of that song, "By A Babbling Brook". And just look at all that thick green foliage, I bet there's loads of rabbits and other wildlife around here.'

'Aye, I think you're right there – they'll probably live in harmony alongside the wild ponies. I'll tell you what, Ernie, the lads back in camp don't know what they're missing, it's great out here on the moor.'

'Talking about camp, John, I think we'd better make our way back now or we might miss out on our grub.'

'Yeah, righto chum – let's go!'

Ernie truly was in peak condition, and a few days later he did something that really put his fitness to the test. The Regimental Sergeant Major was very stringent as far as army rules were concerned, and he came down hard on any soldier who broke them. A pet hate of his was skiving, and he forbade anyone to go to his billet during duty hours. Every day, after an early-morning bugle call, we had to wash, have breakfast, shave and be on duty parade in our full regalia for 0800 hours. From then on no-one was allowed to re-enter his barrack room until midday unless with prior permission. The barracks was a two-storey building and our billet was on the first floor.

On this particular day, Ernie, Jimmy, Brian and I were lurking about in the billet trying to avoid latrine duty. We were acting rather foolishly because the only entrance or exit to the large room was via a flight of stone stairs, which proved to be our undoing.

'What's that noise?' asked Jimmy as we stood around idling.

We all made our way to the landing and Brian peered over a banister only to see the RSM marching into one of the downstairs billets. 'Oh no!' he panicked, 'He's doing one of his flaming on-the-spot inspections!'

'Can we not sneak out now, before he comes out of that room?' asked Jimmy, becoming flustered.

'No way,' said Brian, 'there's a corporal stood on guard at the bottom of the stairs.'

We headed back into the billet but there was nowhere to hide. As I looked around the long room, which was like a hospital ward, we heard the distinct sound of boots clattering up the stone stairs.

'Bloody hell!' exclaimed Brian, 'That's the RSM for sure – we're for the high jump when he catches us!'

'It looks like he's already caught us,' I said. 'The only way out is down those steps that he's coming up.'

That's what I thought, but Ernie had other ideas. 'What are you talking about, John? He'll not catch me – I'm going out of one of the windows! Are you coming?'

'You must be joking!' I grimaced. 'It's a fourteen-foot drop; we could break both our legs, or even be killed!'

'He's right,' Brian and Jimmy responded at the same time.

Ernie took no heed and just said, unconcerned, 'Righto lads, please yourselves, but I'm going.' Without a second thought he opened one of the sliding sash windows and leapt to the parade ground below, leaving Jimmy, Brian and me staring in amazement.

A split second later, the RSM entered, bellowing 'Right, you bunch of lily-livered skivers, you're all on a charge for malingering. Now get your arses out of here down onto that parade ground... *now*! At the double!'

Knowing all too well not to argue with the officer, we scurried down the stairs as fast as we could. When we reached the parade ground, Ernie was strolling about as though nothing had happened.

'See, lads? I told you it was easy,' he whispered. 'It was just like jumping into a swimming pool.'

His voice was overshadowed by the RSM screeching 'Right, you three – get yourselves down to the sergeants' mess and scrub them ablutions until they shine like a new pin! And when you've finished them you can report to the officers' mess and do the same there!' As we were marching off he caught sight of Ernie and beckoned him.

'Right, Sir,' Ernie replied, coming to attention.

'Good man, Private Christie,' asserted the RSM, handing him an envelope. 'Take this letter to the CO's office as quickly as possible, please.'

Ernie took the letter and ran off, but not before glancing at us and giving us a cheeky grin. After that he never let us forget the skirmish and would rib us at every possible opportunity.

Another incident with Ernie was the time he met his future wife in Taunton, a small town 80 miles north of Plymouth in the county of Somerset. A few of us, including Jimmy and Brian, were posted there to erect tents within a Territorial Army campsite on the outskirts of the town. The object was to set up a small field hospital, which would then be used to put on a public exhibition showing how to cope with casualties under war conditions. It was still summer and after a hard day's work we relaxed by having a few drinks in a village pub along with the locals. But Ernie wasn't into this – he didn't want to miss out on the light nights.

'Come on, Ernie,' I pleaded, trying to encourage him. 'We've grafted all day – come join us, we're entitled to a pint.'

'Yeah, I know that, John – but I don't want to miss out on a night like this. I'm going for a run.'

The other lads joined in, trying to make him change his mind. 'Come on, Ernie – lighten up and live a little!' But Ernie was adamant and wouldn't be swayed. 'No, lads, you lighten up your way and I'll do it mine – thanks all the same.'

That was Ernie to a tee. Nevertheless he did succumb on the Saturday night. The village hall was putting on a dance and we were all looking forward to the event.

'Are you coming, Ernie?' we all urged him. 'We know you love to take the fresh air into your lungs, but this is a one-off. We'll never get the chance again!'

'Go on then, you bunch of boozers,' he laughed, 'I'll come if it's the only way to get you lot off my back!'

It must have been fate, because at this particular dance Ernie met the love of his life. When we arrived, music was already playing and the place was typical of any other church hall. The lads were excited because there were lots of pretty girls in the dancehall, but Ernie only had eyes for one of them – we later found out that her name was Maureen. He was very shy and didn't know how to dance, but he did know that he liked this girl. It stood out a mile to me and my mates that he was smitten.

'Go on, Ernie, ask her for a dance,' we all encouraged him, 'you've got nothing to lose! We won't ever be coming back here again.'

'Yeah, I know that, but I've got butterflies in my stomach – I've never taken a lass out before.'

'We're not asking you to take her out – just ask her for a dance, that's all.'

'I know, but I'm scared to death and my knees are shaking. I've never ever felt like this before.'

'It's not like you, Ernie,' Brian remarked. 'You're usually not frightened of anything.'

'Aye, but this is different. I always feel awkward around girls.'

'I'll tell you what, Ernie,' said Jimmy, 'she keeps glancing over here and I'm sure it's you she's looking at.'

'Yeah, I've noticed that too,' said Brian. 'Go on, Ernie – go for it!'

'I don't like…'

Brian cut him short. 'Don't be a wet lettuce! The worst that can happen is she turns you down.'

Jimmy and I continued to encourage him, but it all seemed to fall on deaf ears. Then, out of the blue, after about an hour and a half he finally plucked up the courage. He took a deep breath, stuck out his chest and made his way towards her. Well, that was the last we saw of him that night! They both appeared totally engrossed in each other's company and he never left her side for the rest of the evening.

'Just look at him swooning,' said Brian. 'They seem to be getting on like a house on fire.'

'Aye,' sniggered Jimmy, 'and he doesn't seem to be quaking at the knees anymore!'

I couldn't resist adding 'No, and he's not doing too bad to say he's never had a girl before. Just look at 'em chatting away like bosom buddies.'

At the end of the night, Brian, Jimmy and I were stood by the door when Ernie passed by hand-in-hand with the young girl.

'Did you see that wink he gave us?' said Brian.

'I did that,' said Jimmy, 'we'll never hear the last of it – he'll be like a cat with two tails!'

But in the end, we were all wrong. When we got back to camp Ernie was in bed, tucked up and fast asleep. Next morning we couldn't wait to quiz him on how he'd gone on.

'Great!' he said. 'It was the best night I've ever had. We got on really well and I've got a date with her this afternoon.'

'A date on Sunday afternoon? Where are you going to take her?' I asked.

'Believe it or not,' he grinned, 'she's into keep fit and loves the outdoors. I told her I'm into cross-country running and she said she'd love to come on a ten-mile run with me.'

All three of us started laughing. 'Trust you, Ernie, to come up with something like that!'

It was no laughing matter to Ernie, though; he thought the world of this girl and was determined to make an impression on his first date. The day went well and he took her out one more time before we had to return to Plymouth. But that wasn't the end of the affair. In fact, it was just the beginning. From then on he hitch-hiked the 160 miles from Plymouth to Taunton and back at every opportunity. I'd lost my outdoor partner, but I wasn't bothered – I felt really glad for Ernie.

We didn't realise it then, but after being demobbed Ernie would go to live in Taunton, court the young girl and eventually marry her.

During the next few months the arduous regime continued. I worked in field hospitals, setting up tents on the bleak expanse of Dartmoor. Besides the fieldwork, we did long route marches over the grasslands of the moor, which were criss-crossed with muddy tank tracks. This vast area was made up of peaty soil covered with heather, bracken and moss. On many an occasion, after footslogging until sunset, we just bivouacked down for the night in the middle of nowhere. One day, after traipsing for hours, we had to make our way through a swamp – I didn't need rocking to sleep that night! Other days, dressed in full battle regalia, we spent hours on an Army assault course climbing hanging nets, crawling through muddy pipes on our bellies and negotiating countless other obstacles. Consequently we were in peak condition and ready to be posted anywhere in the world at short notice. In our case it happened to be the Cameroons.

Talk of an uprising had quickly spread throughout the barracks, and within 24 hours the camp was placed on emergency standby. Standing orders notified us that we had to report in batches to the medical centre for inoculations against various tropical diseases. Word spread round the camp that during the First World War, the Cameroons had become known as 'the white man's grave' because so many men had died due to the numerous diseases prominent in that part of the world. A law had since been passed that under no circumstances could any British soldier being shipped out there serve more than nine months. This gave rise to further anxiety.

'Bloomin' 'eck, I'm not looking forward to this.' I muttered as we all queued for the dreaded needles.

'No, neither am I,' whined Rob. 'Why do we have to have 'em anyway?'

'Because you wouldn't last two minutes in Africa, that's why, you bloody dimwit!' rapped a corporal who was standing behind us. 'Especially once you're out in the jungle.'

'I take it you've been abroad before?' I asked.

'Yes, I have, twice in fact... but even I have to have a top-up because there are loads of diseases over there that we're not immune to.'

'How many do we have to have?' asked one rather nervous-looking soldier. 'I can't stand needles! Does it hurt?'

If he was looking for sympathy he didn't get it. 'Three,' scoffed the corporal, 'and yes, it does hurt; they use the bloody longest needles they can find.'

The poor bloke turned as white as a sheet and his distress increased as two other lads teased him.

'I've heard that the vaccine they give you for yellow fever is like treacle and it kills when it's going in!'

'Yeah, and it throbs like mad for hours afterwards, and the one for smallpox is worse than that,' laughed the other.

Others joined in the ribbing and the poor bloke trembled like an aspen. I was anxious as well and had butterflies in my stomach, but I still felt sorry for the lad. However, fate then took a hand. What happened next reminded me of something my dad used to say when I was a young lad. 'What goes round, our John, comes around. Do a bad turn in this life and somewhere along the way it will rebound back onto you.'

Well, it certainly did in this case. The nervous lad had his injections without any undue reactions, whereas the two blokes who had been teasing him flaked out and had to be laid out on a bed. Even the corporal had to sit down on a chair. All the lads laughed as the nervous lad went up to him and said, 'Are you all right, Corporal? Is there anything I can do for you?'

After the ordeal lots of other lads experienced slight reactions and had to retire to their bunks.

Colonel Peck, our commanding officer, granted everyone embarkation leave, but gave strict orders for us to report back to camp at short notice. After being issued with railway travel warrants for the homeward and return journey, we all eagerly made our way to the railway station. I'd been home on leave a few times before but this occasion was different. I was aware that I wouldn't see my family again for some time, but the thought kept crossing my mind that I might never see them again. With that in mind, I was determined to enjoy every minute of my leave at home with my loved ones. In fact, it was during this particular period that I started a relationship with my future wife on a Saturday night in a large dancehall.

I'd spent just a week at home and was thoroughly enjoying myself when I received the order summoning me back to barracks. So here I was heading for Plymouth, full of mixed feelings as the train wheels thundered over the steel tracks. I arrived in Plymouth at seven o'clock that night, giving me ample time to catch the last bus to Crownhill. The camp was bustling with activity and two days later, at two o'clock in the morning, came the final order. We were on our way.

Despite the early hour, excitement reached fever pitch as the storeman kitted us out with tropical gear. Raised voices sounded through the air as 30 soldiers climbed into the back of three Bedford trucks, which were ready to transport us to Southampton Docks. Filled with anticipation, the troops broke into song as we passed through the camp gates, heading in convoy to our destination. Not quite knowing what to expect, once again I felt nervous and uneasy.

'Hey, what's up, John? Are you all right?' asked Brian Holdsworth. 'Your face could stop the town-hall clock.'

'Bloomin' 'eck, Brian! Does it show that much?' I replied, feeling a little embarrassed.

'Aye, it does. I thought you'd have been o'er the moon at going abroad.'

'I am, I am – honest! It's just that I've got bloomin' butterflies in my stomach and I can't shake 'em off.'

'Yeah, so have I, but never mind, eh? We'll feel better once we're on the ship with some ale in our bellies… just you wait and see.'

'Aye, I know we will. Thanks a lot. I didn't realise you were feeling the same as me.'

'I am that, John… Can't you hear my knees knocking?'

'Good lad, Bri. Anyroad, are you gonna give us one of your songs? It'll perk us all up.'

Brian was a big lad, weighing more than 16 stone, but he had the voice of an angel. He was a gentle giant and his voice, like his nature, was soft, sweet and mellow.

A silence descended over the truck as he began to sing:

Ma-ma... I want to tell you that I'll always love you,
Ma-ma, now we're apart I'm always dreaming of you.
I think of the days when I was just a kid,
We were so happy together.
Who cared for me with such tenderness,
No one my darling but you.
Ma-ma, oh how I miss you now that we are apart,
Ma-ma... so wonderful,
You'll always find a place in my heart,
My Ma-ma... my own...

You could hear a pin drop as he sang. I looked around at the expressions on the men's faces – men from London, Birmingham, Liverpool, Manchester, Scotland and other places. They were down-to-earth men, tough as nails, but as Brian sang in his sensitive, touching way, tears welled up in their eyes and rolled down their cheeks – and I was no exception. It got me thinking that there's no one like your mam when you're away from home.

I perked up a little when I became aware that I wasn't the only one feeling jittery. A tingling sensation ran down my spine as I looked at these men, all unashamed. I realised that they, too, were feeling melancholy. It was a source of comfort and somehow made me feel more secure.

CHAPTER TWO
THE *DEVONSHIRE*

The quayside was chaotic, with hundreds of soldiers milling around. Kitbags, ship provisions and the baggage that accompanies all armies were lying in great big heaps. Men were shouting and whistles were blowing. Order, the main characteristic of Army life, seemed to have broken down. All this activity took place in the cover of our ship, the *Devonshire*, which loomed like a leviathan waiting to devour the agitated, ant-like throng scurrying around in its mighty shadow, waiting patiently to create order out of chaos.

As we alighted from the back of the truck, soldiers were darting hither and thither among the hustle and bustle, trying to organise themselves. Amid the confusion I dropped my kitbag right into the path of a burly sergeant.

'Pick that up on the double, soldier!' he bellowed, his handlebar moustache twitching.

'Right, Sergeant,' I replied, not wanting to get on the wrong side of him.

'What regiment are you from?' he barked.

'The medics,' I spluttered, clutching my kitbag and feeling like Stan Laurel.

'The medics? I might have known... The Girl Guides have arrived, have they?'

The remark raised a few eyebrows among my mates, but as he was a sergeant it was ignored. Name-calling and barracking was something the Medical Corps had to put up with. It had been a regular occurrence at Seaton Barracks and many a fight with other regiments had ensued. However, most medics could handle themselves and we had gradually gained the respect of our peers. But that was back in Plymouth – it now appeared that we would have to go through the same rigmarole all over again.

'It looks like we'll have to stick together, lads,' said Brian, addressing all the medics. 'At least till we get to know them, and them us.'

'You should have told that bloody sergeant to get lost!' snarled Ken Smith, venting his anger at me.

'Oh yeah, sure... like you would have done!' I snapped back.

'What do you mean by that, Cowell?'

'I mean what I say, Smithy!'

'Come on, lads,' put in Jimmy, acting as peacemaker. 'Let's

not fall out among ourselves. Like big Brian said, we've got to rally together and watch each other's backs – you know the score.'

'You're right, Jimmy,' I replied. 'I'm willing to let it go if you are, Ken. How about it?'

'Aye, 'course I am, John. Sorry for opening my gob in the first place. Let's shake on it,' he said, reaching out his hand, 'and put it down to nerves.'

'Cheers, Ken,' I responded, offering my hand.

While waiting to board the gigantic monster, my mates and I put our kitbags on the ground and sat on them.

'Blimey,' spluttered Rob, taken aback by the immense size of the ship. 'How the flamin' 'eck can something like that float? It beats me.'

'That's what I was thinking,' added Bri. 'It's solid steel and must weigh a million tons.'

'Come on, Bri – what did you expect to carry a battalion of soldiers?' quipped Jimmy. 'A flamin' rowing boat?'

'Good one, Jimmy. You'll make a comedian one of these days.'

A wave of silence descended on the docks as a distorted voice came over an antiquated loudspeaker, dishing out orders for everyone to board the ship.

'Let's hang about for a little bit longer,' put in Brian. 'Those orders are just for the infantry mob. We may as well wait until most of the commotion has settled down.'

That's what he thought, but our little break didn't last long before it was interrupted by the same snotty sergeant.

'Come on, girls! Get your arses onto that bloody gangplank now – at the double!'

Bri and Ken nearly rose to the bait but knew better than to get involved. I was tempted to ask Ken why he hadn't said anything to the sergeant but thought it would be better left alone.

As we made our way up the gangplank of the great ship our studded boots clattered loudly on the steel deck and metal staircases. It put me in mind of when I was a little boy in junior school. My schoolmates and I always wore steel-bottomed clogs, which made a distinctive sound in the schoolyard, which was made of concrete.

I couldn't help but think of a couple of lines from a poem that I had once written:

'Paraded like soldiers dressed in our togs,
Clip clop, clip clop went the sound of our clogs.'

Our little group of medics gathered together for moral support on the deck's port side, awaiting further orders. We were dwarfed by 600 troops from the King's Own Border Regiment and other attachments such as the Royal Electrical Mechanical Engineers (REME), the Catering Corps, the Signals and the Royal Army Service Corps (RASC). We even had some ladies from the Queen Alexandra Royal Army Nursing Corps (QUARANCS).

It soon became evident that they weren't well liked in Army circles because of their supercilious State Registered Nurse behaviour. Most of them were newly enlisted young women who had just recently qualified. The reason for their haughty manner was mainly due to their protective rank. On enrolment into the Army they were given the rank of second lieutenant, whereas a man with the same qualification was only made a sergeant – three steps lower in the ranking ladder. But the main difference was that a sergeant came under the status of non-commissioned officer, whereas a second lieutenant was a commissioned officer who had to be saluted. This instant leap to status appeared to trigger off conceit.

I'd had a run-in with them during my training days for not saluting one of them in passing. She immediately took offence and after dressing me down, put me on a charge. I got three days' jankers. This was the term given to extra fatigues over and above the normal chores of a working day, plus confinement to camp. And I wasn't the only one – the same thing happened to a few of my mates. It didn't take long for soldiers to refer to the high and mighty women as snotty-nosed bitches and other choice names.

On the *Devonshire* there were 20 troops to every medic, which was rather daunting, but they turned out to be a friendly bunch and we soon became one big happy family. Under the circumstances, common sense prevailed. We were all being shipped off to a war-torn country and knew only too well that our very lives depended on each other down to the last man – it was reminiscent of the comradeship I had experienced while working in the coalmines.

Within two hours the last rope had dropped from its mooring and the ship started to stir as its massive engines roared into action, edging slowly away from the quayside. The ship was huge, and as I stood holding the rail, it made me feel small and vulnerable. As I looked down, I wondered how many young soldiers had left this dock in the past and never returned. I quickly dismissed this thought from my mind because I didn't want to dwell on it; I was jittery enough as it was.

There was no one on the dockside to wave us off, but we all felt it was a memorable occasion as a strange, wonderful silence descended onto the deck. The ambience spread throughout the entire ship, rendering all the men passive and mellow.

It put me in mind of a similar experience when I was a young boy of six. It was announced over the wireless one evening that Germany had surrendered and that the war in Europe, which had lasted six long years, was over. Spontaneously, hordes of neighbours from every household, many in their nightclothes, gathered on the front street to celebrate the joyous occasion. Within minutes the crowd swelled to hundreds as more people flocked from other streets, all making their way to town. Many were carrying flags and other decorations, which they'd stored in their bottom drawers in readiness for such an occasion.

'Where are you all going?' my dad asked inquisitively.

'We're going to the town hall to have a right rave up,' a few answered in unison. 'So get your glad rags on and come and join us!'

'Too true I will,' he responded. And turning to us, 'Come on, kids, go and get your coats on, this is something we don't want to miss!' So, I, along with my dad and my brothers and sisters, followed these happy souls. The festivities were unforgettable as flags soon festooned the streets and thousands of happy people danced merrily away to the sound of brass bands, the clashing of dustbin lids and men playing mouth organs. Crowds of people linked up together, while others danced the conga. An indelible impression was stamped onto my young mind. Just as now, a huge crowd was thronged, mainly outside the town hall, and as the big clock struck twelve everyone sank spontaneously into the same indescribable silence as if synchronised from above.

My thoughts were interrupted as big Brian started to sing:

Now is the hour for me to say goodbye,
Soon I'll be sailing far across the sea.
While I'm away,
Please remember me!

After clearing our throats we all joined in, singing in harmony with Brian. It was the strangest of feelings to hear the melodious voices of hundreds of young men tuned in as if in a choir, making the atmosphere sublime. The singing continued as we steamed slowly from Southampton into the Solent, where we espied the Isle of Wight in all its glory. It was shrouded in mist, but still looked beautiful. As the ship steered slowly through the cold waters of the English Channel, the first leg of our 3,000-mile journey, we all seemed to unite, forming a bond with each other.

We were soon brought back to reality. We'd hardly put out to

sea before various corporals started yelling out orders for us all
to fall into different ranks on the main deck. One of them,
Corporal Murphy, took charge of our small group and
shepherded us in single file down some steel staircases to a long
confined section of the ship, which contained three-tier steel
bunk beds on either side of a narrow aisle. He seemed to gloat as
he then pointed out that this was our sleeping quarters.

'Flamin' 'eck,' grunted Jimmy Mitchinson. 'This is like being
on a submarine!'

It was, too – right in the very heart of the ship, with portholes
the only source of natural light. I got an instant feeling of
claustrophobia, more so than I'd ever experienced while working
down the coalmine.

'Crikey!' I thought. 'I don't fancy sleeping in this chicken coop
for the next three weeks. There's not enough room to swing a
cat.' But my thoughts were interrupted by the bawling corporal.
'Right, you scruffy lot! As far as some places are concerned, this
is The Ritz. Make the best of it, because this is as good as it gets!'

'You must be joking like,' said Mick, a Liverpudlian. 'I've got a
dog back 'ome that sleeps in better conditions than these.'

'Oh, have you now?' the quick-witted corporal replied. 'Well,
let me tell you – when you've finished your stint in the Army you
can go back and sleep with your dog, but while you're here, this
is where you'll kip. Anyway, like I said, it doesn't get any better,
and until we reach Africa this is going to be home sweet home. So
don't forget to keep the place tidy, and that includes making up
your bunks every morning.'

'Oh aye, and what about you?' asked Jimmy. 'I suppose you've got a room all to yourself?'

'Ha, ha, ha!' the corporal laughed. 'I can assure you I don't get special treatment because of my stripes. There's only one bloke who gets a room of his own on a troop ship and that's the captain. If it makes you feel any better, that's my bed over there, the first on the left.'

After giving us a few more instructions his attitude became much friendlier and he even displayed a witty sense of humour, creating a good atmosphere. Eventually our 'chicken coop' took on a different light. Corporal Murphy was in his mid-thirties and a regular soldier with 15 years' service under his belt. It soon became evident that his nickname was Spud – and that he was an alcoholic. His favourite breakfast was two cans of beer, and when he stripped off, he revealed two tattoos on his chest – the word 'mild' under his left nipple and 'bitter' beneath his right one.

'Right, Brian,' I said, after packing my meagre belongings into a small bedside locker. 'I'm going on a walkabout to discover the layout of the ship – how about you?'

'Aye, righto. It'll be good to get a breather after being stifled down here.'

'I'll come with you as well,' said Jimmy. 'Anything to get out of this rat hole.'

When we reached the deck we were well out at sea and England's shoreline was barely visible.

As I stood clutching the rails a fear of the unknown enveloped me. Once again I started to panic and a shiver ran down my spine.

'I wonder if I'll ever see home again?' I mumbled to myself. I wondered how many of my mates were feeling the same. Though I tried in vain to dispel these pessimistic thoughts from my head, try as I might they just wouldn't go away. I felt ashamed, as though I was acting cowardly.

Then, right out of the blue, my guardian angel came to my rescue. The burly sergeant who had shouted his mouth off on the docks came and stood near me, grasping the steel rails. At first I felt uneasy but then I noticed that he seemed somewhat anxious. His whole demeanour was different as he gripped the rails tightly and swayed backwards and forwards. His twitchy demeanour urged me to look closer and I was shocked to see a little tear rolling down his cheek. It made me realise that he was feeling the same natural emotions as me.

That's it! I thought. If a veteran experienced soldier like him can feel the pressure, it's no wonder that I feel agitated.

'Are you all right, John?' asked Jimmy, tapping me on the shoulder. 'You seem miles away.'

'Yeah, sorry... I was feeling a bit jittery but I'm all right now.'

'Tell me about it!' he laughed. 'So are me and Brian.'

Just then we heard lots of happy voices.

'Where's all that coming from?' asked Brian.

'I don't know, but let's go and find out, eh?'

We headed across the deck towards the sound and as we drew near to a doorway, we could hear lots of raucous laughter. To our delight we found lots of lads drinking and smoking in a large concert room, which housed a long bar.

'Yippee! I'm into that,' said Brian. 'How about you, John?'

'Too true, Bri lad. Like you said when we were on the dockside – we'll feel a lot better once we get some ale in our bellies.'

As I approached the bar I met two mates from my home town who were serving in other regiments. The first was Martin Grogan, which wasn't surprising because I'd had a night out with him while home on embarkation leave and was expecting to see him on the ship.

'Hiya, Johnny. I've been keeping my eyes peeled for you. I'd an idea I might find you in here.'

'Great to see you, Martin. The last time we met was down the Nelson Imp, wasn't it? I lost you in the crowd once we got inside the ballroom.'

'Aye, it was heaving, wasn't it? What a great night!'

'It was that. How did you go on?'

'Superb. I met a lass called Mary Smith and I took her to the pictures the following night.'

'Oh aye? Go on, tell me more.'

'Well, I liked her and we had a couple more dates and decided to write to each other while I'm in the Cameroons. Anyroad, how did you fare?'

'Well, believe it or not, a similar thing happened to me. There was a girl in the dancehall called Edna Simpson, whom I've fancied for ages but never had the courage to ask her for a dance. But that night I thought it'd be stupid not to, 'cos I knew I wouldn't be back in England for a while. I took her out on the Sunday night and twice after that, and we decided to keep in touch while I'm in Africa.'

'Good lad, John. Come on, let's drink to it.'

'Yeah, I'll go along with that. Are you having a pint?'

'No pints on this ship, John – they only have cans.'

'Whatever, as long as it's ale I don't mind. Anyroad, Martin, this is my mate Brian from Leeds,' I said, as Brian edged his way to the bar.

'By 'eck, Brian, you're a big lad. I wouldn't like to get on the wrong side of you! Anyroad, pleased to meet you – any friend of John is a friend o' mine.'

'All I can say to that,' Brian laughed, 'is you're not very choosy about the company you keep, are you? Anyway, what are you drinking? I'll get these.'

'Cheers! I'll have a can o' lager.'

We were drinking away happily when things got even better.

'Hiya Johnny,' called a voice from behind me. 'I never expected to see you on this ship.' On turning I saw it was Neville Atkinson, a friend of mine who'd been in the same class as me at Towneley Technical High School.

'All right, Nev!' I spluttered in disbelief. 'How's it going? Are you with the King's Own Borderers?'

'No, but I'm attached to them. I'm in the Signals. And you, what company are you with?'

'The medics.'

'Oh, the cushy mob,' he laughed.

'So they say, Nev, so they say... We'll have to wait and see. Ask me again in six months' time and I'll tell you then. Anyroad, it can't be any cushier than being in the Signals.'

'Yeah, you could be right there, John… I hope so.'

'Are you joining us, Nev?' asked Martin, who also knew him from back home.

'Yeah, why not? In for a penny, in for a pound, as they say.'

As the merriment continued, the conversation turned to the duty-free prices.

'This is great!' laughed one of the infantry lads, holding a can of ale in one hand and a canister of cigarettes in the other. 'Fifty fags for half a dollar and Senior Service at that.'

'Blimey!' said another lad. 'That works out at only about ha'penny each.'

I couldn't help thinking that my dad would have lapped this up and been in his glory.

'I think I'm going to like being on this boat,' put in Martin, with a grin on his face.

'Aye, so am I,' said big Bri. 'Cheap fags and cheap booze… great, isn't it?'

'I don't know so much,' I said. 'It seems too good to be true. I can't see it lasting… There's gotta be a snag somewhere.'

'Don't put a damper on it, John,' he laughed. 'Enjoy it while you can… make hay while the sun shines.'

'John may be right,' cautioned Martin. 'I can't see this lasting the duration of the voyage; they're bound to come up with something. Anyway, what about guard duty and fatigues?'

'Don't worry about that,' said an older regular soldier from the next table. 'I've been on a troopship loads o' times afore and it's the life o' Riley. You've got to keep your bunk tidy and do some physical training on the main deck every morning, but that's about it.'

'Surely someone's got to do guard duty or kitchen fatigues?' I asked.

'Aye, that's true but that's left to the infantry mob.'

'Great!' chorused Brian, Neville and me.

Martin wasn't so enthusiastic. 'Bloomin' 'eck! That means that I might cop for it.'

'Aye, if you're unlucky,' replied the regular soldier. 'Anyhow, even if you do, you'll only have to do one stint at the most 'cos there's 600 men to share it. The rest of the time you can sunbathe, play games, drink or whatever takes your fancy. Like I said, it's a great life.'

'U-um, that'll do me,' I giggled inwardly. I was happy, but I made a pact to keep myself in good shape with regular daily exercises. It would be easy to become complacent and fall into the trap of self-indulgence with all the cheap ale and fags about.

My mind went back to when I first joined the Army. Out of my meagre allowance of 25 shillings I'd allotted seven to my mam back home. In return for this the Army made it up and granted Mum a pension of £3 10s a week for the duration of my time in Her Majesty's Forces. But the Army also had a policy whereby they paid out to the nearest five shillings, putting the remainder into 'credits'. I didn't mind this, as it was a kind of saving-up scheme, which I could call upon if need be. But it also meant I was left with only a paltry 15 shillings in my hand, from which I had to buy toothpaste, razor blades, soap or whatever. Consequently,

I could only afford to go out for a drink on payday and had to scrimp and for the rest of the week.

After six months' service I got a rise of 10 shillings, which eased the burden somewhat. Then, after serving 12 months, I had a further 10-shilling rise. This coincided with being shipped off to Africa, which meant that I received an additional bonus in the guise of an overseas allowance. I was now on nearly £4 a week – I felt like Rothschild.

After our drinking session we all returned to our sleeping quarters only to find that they didn't appear quite so dingy any more. Whether it was the effects of the beer I don't know, but they now looked all right to me and I was asleep within five minutes of getting into my bunk. Next morning I awoke to the sound of a few lads making their way to the washroom, while most of the others were still in bed snoring away.

Oh boy, this is great! I thought. Life on the ocean waves… I don't think I'm going to miss dear old Blighty after all.

Jimmy Mitchinson, who bunked in the bed above mine, was beginning to stir. 'All right, John? What time is it?' he groaned, clutching his forehead.

'Eight o'clock. Are you coming for breakfast?'

'U-ugh, forget it! I've got the ding-dong of all hangovers.'

'Right, I'll see you later then.'

I didn't ask Brian if he was coming because he was sleeping like a baby. I hadn't drunk quite as much as them, and besides, breakfast was one of my favourite meals. Dinner and tea were favourites too… I loved my grub.

At ten o'clock, just like the regular soldier had told us, we all had to report to the main deck for a session of physical training. After the workout, a voice sounded over a loud speaker bringing us to attention, whereupon the commanding officer addressed us from the ship's bridge:

'Right, gentlemen – you all seem to be enjoying yourselves and that's the way I want it to be for the next two weeks until we reach our destination. But I give you fair warning: don't abuse my hospitality. I need you all to be in prime condition when we reach the Cameroons. First of all, there will be a roll call on deck every morning to make sure no one has fallen overboard. During the voyage, other than physical training and attending educational lectures, you will only have light duties to perform, so I want you all to feel relaxed. Mind you, you may have other menial tasks to perform, should the need arise.

'But I'm not a soft touch and I won't tolerate any indiscipline. You may wear shorts and strip down to the waist for comfort once we reach warmer waters. But take heed! Anyone who gets sunburned is liable to finish up on a charge. If any one of you finishes up in sick bay due to sunstroke, you'll lose your pay and time spent there will be added onto your length of service.

'Another thing: I expect you all to comply with Army regulations regarding personal hygiene – this includes having a shave every morning. Furthermore, despite the relaxation of duties, remember you are still in the Army and under orders from your direct superiors, so behave accordingly. Finally, I would just like to say enjoy it while it lasts, because once we reach the Cameroons you'll wonder what's hit you!'

On that note he dismissed everyone, and loud cheering echoed throughout the ship as the message was received in high spirits.

'I'll tell you what, John,' said Jimmy. 'I'm gonna enjoy this voyage. It's like being on a cruise… all at Her Majesty's expense.'

'Yeah, me too,' chipped in a few of the other lads.

Well, that was it. We really did have a good time over the following two weeks, lazing about on deck, swimming in the small pool or anything else that took our fancy… Life was great!

One incident involving Rob and the troop deck sergeant had us all in stitches. It started because the non-commissioned officer was the spitting image of Private Doberman from the popular television series *Sergeant Bilko*. The troop deck sergeant not only looked like his famous counterpart facially and bodily, he also tended to have similar funny mannerisms.

Rob and I were so used to hearing him referred to as Doberman that we actually thought it was his real name. Consequently, one day Rob dropped a clanger that raised a few laughs and got us out of a spot of bother at the same time.

Deck games and indoor sports such as table tennis were encouraged during the voyage. Snooker, darts and cards were also played in the concert room, but gambling was strictly forbidden. Still, this pastime did take place, but mainly on the troop decks away from the watchful eyes of our superiors. This particular incident came about while we were idling our time away.

Rob came up with a suggestion: 'I've got some spare cash just burning a hole in my pocket, John. Let's go and join the lads below deck for a gambling session.'

'Yeah, why not? We may get into trouble but sod it!'

So, regardless of the consequences, off we went. We soon became involved in a session of three-card brag and after 20 minutes I was quite excited, as I was £3 up. But my enthusiasm came to an abrupt end as one of the lads on lookout raised the alarm.

'Watch out! Two officers coming!'

Panicking, we got rid of the cards, stuffing some under the mattresses and others into bedside lockers. Within moments Captain Gedding and Lieutenant Olsen were upon us.

'What's going on here?' rapped the captain.

Rob was the nearest person to him and he started blabbering that we had been discussing what life would be like in the Cameroons.

'Don't give me that,' the officer snapped. 'I'm not falling for that rubbish!'

'But sir...' stammered Rob, striving to come up with an excuse.

'Never mind trying to bluff your way out of it, soldier. I wasn't born yesterday. Anyway, who's your troop sergeant?'

'Troop Sergeant Doberman,' replied Bob, much to the lads' amusement.

'Troop Sergeant Doberman?' queried the captain, looking puzzled. 'I've never heard of him.' Turning to Lieutenant Olsen he asked, 'Do you know this Sergeant Doberman?'

Furrowing his brows, the lieutenant answered, 'No, I don't. I haven't a clue... he's definitely not an infantryman, maybe he's a medic.'

'This Sergeant Doberman,' the captain asked Rob, 'is he a medic and what's he like?'

By this time my mates were all looking at the ground, trying their hardest not to laugh. At first I wondered what they found so amusing and then suddenly it became clear – especially when Rob started to describe the man.

'Well, sir, he's little and stubby, and has a round face with a kind of cheesy grin, and he talks with a squeaky voice.'

I realised that the captain had clicked on, as I noticed a smirk at the corner of his mouth.

'O-oh, Sergeant Doberman... I know who you mean now,' he smiled. Turning again to the other officer he asked, 'And you, Lieutenant Olsen – do *you* know who he means now?'

'I certainly do,' he replied, trying to suppress a giggle.

The funniest part was that by now everybody had cottoned on.... except Rob. At least it defused the situation and, instead of putting us all on a charge, the captain let us off with a caution. 'I'll let it go this time, lads, but don't let me catch any one of you gambling again or so help me, I'll throw the book at you!'

'Ha ha ha, that was a good one, Rob!' all the lads roared. 'Sergeant *Doberman*! Where the bloody hell did you dig that up from?'

'Dig it up from? What are you talking about?' asked the bewildered Rob. 'Is that not his name then?'

That triggered the lads off again. Everyone was in stitches, including me.

'Come on, John – what's so funny? I don't get it!'

'Oh, come off it, Rob,' I stuttered in between gusts of laughter. 'You're not usually so thick. The TV show – *Sergeant Bilko and Doberman* – you know what I mean.'

At last the penny dropped. To give him his due, though, even Rob saw the funny side of it. For days after we all had a good laugh at his expense – especially when Troop Sergeant Doberman strutted around the deck.

It was on the *Devonshire* that I had my first taste of curry. The cooks, all of Chinese origin, specialised in oriental dishes and spicy foods.

'I fancy trying a curry today, John,' said Bri. 'How about you?'

'Not on your life,' was my instant response. 'I've heard they can burn a hole right through your stomach.'

'Don't be so soft! I've been told they're really tasty. Anyroad, when in Rome do as the Romans do, that's what I think.'

'In that case you try it. I'll stick to fish and chips, and sod the Romans!'

'I might just do that. Anyroad, how can you knock what you've never tried?'

'Maybe I haven't but I know some lads who have and they were sick afterwards.'

'Please yourself, John, but I'm gonna have some anyway.'

True to his word he did try some and surprisingly he loved it;

from then on it became his favourite meal. It got me thinking that perhaps I should try it too – maybe I was missing out. So I did try what seemed an exotic dish at the time and discovered it really was tasty. I only had mild ones at first but quickly acquired a taste for the hotter ones – they certainly got to my taste buds. From then on I had a curry dish whenever it was on the menu, and the spicier the better. Those oriental cooks certainly had the knack of conjuring up superb dishes.

But cooking wasn't their only speciality, as we found out to our benefit. Every evening they would parade about the decks shouting, 'D'hobi, d'hobi, anyone for d'hobi?'

'What are they on about, Bri?' I asked, as loads of lads joined in the chorus.

'I don't know. Let's go and find out.'

'D'hobi,' explained a regular soldier, 'means washing. If you've any dirty clothes that need washing, they'll do it for you quite cheap.'

It was, too. Jimmy, Bri and I mustered up a bundle between us and it only cost two shillings.

'Hey, this is great!' said Bri when we got our clothes back. 'They're really clean.'

So, for obvious reasons, the Chinese were soon nicknamed The D'hobi Men.

It was a mild August night when we left Southampton docks and sailed towards the open waters of the Atlantic Ocean, but within a few days the temperature began to rise steadily. The passage was quite smooth until we reached the Bay of Biscay, where the waters became choppy with huge powerful waves driving onto the deck. Despite its size, the *Devonshire* bobbed up and down like a cork on the vast ocean. It wasn't as bad as I expected it to be, but many of the men were lying on their bunks due to terrible seasickness. Others were being violently sick over the side of the boat. My stomach felt queasy and gurgled a little, but other than that I felt fine.

In fact, I actually enjoyed the crossing, as it gave me a feeling of being superhuman. Unlike many other lads, who'd had a skinful of ale the previous day, I hadn't touched a drop. I couldn't settle in the sleeping quarters as they stank, with ashen-faced bodies lying on their bunks and the foul smell of putrefied beer, sick and farts drifting into my nostrils. I couldn't stand the stench so I decided to go up on deck for a breath of fresh air.

I stayed well away from the rails for fear of being washed overboard, and clung tightly to palings of central structures. The immense power of nature thrilled me as the wind whipped up gigantic waves and sea spray lashed into my face, making me feel fresh and rejuvenated. One mighty wave hit me so hard I almost lost my grasp. But still I was undeterred – in fact it made me more determined to ride the mild storm. I imagined I was a crimson pirate as the refreshing feeling invigorated me – I felt vibrant and alive.

Most lads couldn't eat anything but I never missed a meal.

'It's time for some grub, lads,' I laughed to Jimmy and Bri, who were both sprawled out on their bunks.

'Ar-rgh! How you can eat anything is beyond me,' moaned big Bri. 'I feel like I'm dying.'

'Yeah, me too,' groaned Jimmy. 'Let us die in peace.'

'Please yourself,' I joked. 'Are you sure you don't want me to fetch you a fatty bacon butty or something?'

'Get out of here, you bloody sadist!' they screeched, 'before we strangle you!'

'I'm going! I'm going!'

After crossing the Bay of Biscay, the wind settled and the waters calmed down. After we'd sighted the coast of northern Spain the weather improved daily, and from then on the sun shone brightly in a clear blue sky and reflected in the most vivid turquoise sea I'd ever seen in my life. To my sheer delight a shoal of dolphins started to follow the boat, diving in and out of the ocean waves. The frolicking of these wonderful creatures was a sight to behold. I couldn't help but think of God and the beauty of nature. The sheer magnificence of it all astounded me, taking me back in awe.

'How anyone cannot believe in the Almighty when they see such wonders is beyond me,' I thought, as some sea spray gently splashed my face. I've always counted myself lucky because never in my life have I doubted the existence of God or the life hereafter, and at that very moment I felt His presence all around me.

Sailing by the shores of Portugal the ocean appeared even bluer, and against the backdrop of the coastline, it stood out like a beautiful painting. As I strolled around the deck, Martin and Neville were sprawled out soaking up the hot sun.

'This is great, John. You can't beat it!' smiled Martin, peering over his sunglasses.

'Well, it definitely beats working down the pit,' I said. 'I can't get over the colour of the sea – it's so blue and absolutely stunning.'

'Yeah, it is, isn't it? It's like being in a dream.'

'You can say that again!' laughed Bri, arriving on the scene, 'I feel like I'm in Paradise – I've never had it so good.'

He was right too. Everything was perfect – and to top it all, we had money in our pockets.

'Are you going to join us, Bri?' asked Martin. 'This is the life!'

'I sure am,' he answered, stripping down to his shorts.

'Be careful lads,' I warned. 'You know what the CO said about getting sunburned!'

Just then someone tapped me on the shoulder. When I turned around it was Ted Bennett, another lad from Burnley. I'd met Ted 11 years earlier in a convalescent home in Blackpool, where I'd spent two weeks with my older brother Jimmy. It was a home for underprivileged children and Mum had arranged it with the school authorities. It was the one and only time I'd ever been on any kind of holiday and I loved it, especially playing in the sand dunes on the seashore. As it happened, Ted was there with his younger brother Alan, and as the two boys were in a similar situation to ours, we hit it off right from the start. After our little vacation, as the years passed into adulthood, we'd always acknowledged each other whenever out on the social scene.

'Hiya, Johnny! Long time, no see,' Ted greeted me. 'I never expected to see you on this boat.'

'No, you neither, Ted. Which regiment are you with?'

'I'm in the infantry, the same as Martin.'

After going through the same rigmarole as I had with Neville, I had to smile. 'I'll tell you what, Ted – us Burnley-ites will be taking the ship over if they don't watch it.'

'You could be right there,' he laughed. 'Anyroad, at this rate those bloomin' guerillas in the Cameroons had better watch out.'

At that we all started laughing. By now I had really settled in, with no more nerves or anxiety about what lay in store for us, just contentment.

'I believe the entertainment committee is putting on a good show in the hall tonight,' said Ted. 'Is everybody going?'

'Yeah, why not?' we all agreed. 'It'll make a change from boozing.'

It turned out to be a great night with all the acts being performed by soldiers. Some lads had worked in amateur dramatics prior to receiving their conscription papers, but most were from ordinary working-class backgrounds. One lad stood out from the rest; he was a born comedian with a dynamic sense of humour and had us all in stitches – we nicknamed him 'Clowney'.

At the end of the show they put on a talent competition, inviting anyone to join in. Brian sang a medley of songs and went down a treat, coming in second to Clowney. He touched the heartstrings of all the soldiers as he sang tender love songs with tears rolling down his cheeks. Once he started to sing, a quietness descended around the room. He'd just got married before being

45

called up into the Army, and he was terribly lovesick for his new bride. All the lads used to take the mickey out of him, but no matter, every time a love song came over the radio, the tears would appear. Despite his big, bulky frame, he was one of the most sensitive blokes around and as he was also one of the friendliest, he became very popular among the troops.

Someone volunteered my services so I sang a couple of songs from the musical *South Pacific*, which I'd recently seen in Plymouth. In the film, Mitzi Gaynor had dressed up as a sailor and sang 'Honey Bun'. I liked the song and sang it while Clowney pranced about the floor wearing a hula-hula skirt and waggling his hips. I didn't win any prizes but the lads seemed to enjoy it and so did I.

CHAPTER THREE

A SPELL IN THE BRIG

Despite the comradeship and harmony among the men the odd fight was inevitable, due mainly to the effects of alcohol and bravado. In most cases the arguments were sorted out by the intervention of other soldiers who didn't want things to get out of hand. After the two opponents had cooled down they usually shook hands and the matter was forgotten; otherwise, for further entertainment, it was sorted out in a boxing ring. Even so, on one occasion two really powerfully-built chaps got to brawling on the deck, and it became so aggressive that the other lads couldn't control it. Chairs, tables and bits of broken glasses lay strewn all over the place. The military police soon arrived on the scene and the two offenders got marched off to the ship's jail – the brig.

The next day they appeared before the commanding officer on a charge of disruption, the destruction of property and fighting, and he sentenced them both to seven days' detention in the cells with loss of pay. To most soldiers, the loss of pay was more of a deterrent than the actual imprisonment.

When I heard the outcome it took my mind back to a few months earlier, when I'd received the same sentence for disobeying an order at Seaton Barracks in Plymouth. Just a few days prior to my sentence, Colonel Peck, the commandant, had sentenced me to three days' jankers for not polishing my cap badge properly. I didn't question his decision because I was guilty of this trivial offence and felt I could do the jankers stood on my head. I had to report to the orderly sergeant's office at 1900 hours and do two hours' work in the officers' mess. This didn't cause me any concern, but what did was the confinement to camp, whereby I had to report back to the orderly sergeant at 2300 hours before going to bed. The first two nights, Monday and Tuesday, didn't bother me, but having to check in on Wednesday did.

Soldiers completing their two-year stint in the Army always got demobbed on a Thursday, and as Wednesday was payday, a leaving celebration would invariably take place that night in the Cherry Tree, a pub near the town centre that often used to give soldiers a good send-off. On this particular Thursday a friend of mine, Colin, was due to be discharged and I didn't want to miss out on the festivities.

As it happened the orderly sergeant in charge on that Wednesday night was Barry Smith, a lad who had joined the Army the same day as I did. He was a qualified pharmacist, which automatically entitled him to be made up to the rank of sergeant on enlistment. When I reported to him at 1900 hours, I mentioned how I felt about my mate's farewell do.

'E-eh, I'll tell you what, Barry,' I moaned. 'I'm really pissed off about not going to Colin's send-off party. We've been buddies since the first day I arrived here in Plymouth. I don't mind having to wash all the greasy junk, but having to report back here at 2300 hours is a real bind.'

'I know how you feel, John, but there's not a right lot I can do about it. I will say, though, they're having a special do in the officers' mess tonight, so there'll be a mountain of pots and pans to wash. If you get through the lot, I'm willing to turn a blind eye if you don't report to me tonight. Mind you, if anything goes wrong, on your own head be it!'

I didn't need telling twice. As far as I was concerned, a nod was as good as a wink.

Great, I said to myself, looking at the enormous task in front of me. Just watch me get through this lot! I rolled up my sleeves and worked furiously until I'd cleaned the last spoon, finishing on the stroke of nine. Without giving it a second thought, I then ran all the way to the Cherry Tree.

Colin was glad to see me but a little surprised. 'How have you managed it, John? You're supposed to report back to the orderly sergeant at 2300 hours, aren't you?'

'Not to worry, Colin,' I reassured him. 'I've sorted it.'

'All right, John?' asked Bri. 'What are *you* doing here?'

After explaining the situation to him we got down to some serious drinking and singing, and by the end of the night we were all three sheets to the wind.

'I hope you'll be OK, mate,' said Colin as we made our way back to camp. 'I'd hate to think you got into trouble on my behalf.'

'Don't worry about it, Colin. Sergeant Smith said he would turn a blind eye, so I should be all right.'

I couldn't have been more wrong! As we walked through the camp gates I was singled out by the military police.

'What's your name and rank, soldier?' rapped a brawny corporal, towering over me.

'Cowell, Private Cowell,' I answered, knowing full well that something was amiss.

'Private Cowell *what*, soldier!'

'Oh, Private Cowell... Corporal!'

'Attention!' he screeched. 'Get your arse into the guardroom at the double, you slimy little creep! Quick march! Left right, left right!'

This particular MP (Military Police officer) was notorious for putting prisoners under his charge through hell. He stood over six feet tall and as he yelled through bared teeth he looked awesome. He delighted in grinding men into the ground and for a moment his overbearing presence intimidated me.

As soon as I entered the guardroom I saw Sergeant Smith sitting at a table, looking rather sheepish. By his side sat the Regimental Sergeant Major, who was fuming. I had to stand to attention in front of them both.

'Right, Private Cowell, I'm charging you for being absent without leave,' rapped the RSM.

'But, sir...'

'No buts! I made a flying visit to the orderly sergeant's office at 2300 hours and you didn't report there, and it's come to my attention that you left the camp without permission.'

I didn't say much, as I was in a Catch-22 situation. It seemed fruitless to protest because, after all, Sergeant Smith had left the decision with me. I couldn't allow myself to bring his name into it; that wouldn't have been the right thing to do. And anyway, I couldn't come up with anything that would have made a difference. So I said nothing.

'Right, Private Cowell, you're on a charge and you'll appear in front of Colonel Peck at 0900 hours. If you're one minute late you'll be in even more trouble than you are right now! Understood?'

'Yes, sir.'

Turning to the MP he rapped, 'Right – take him away! Get him out of my sight!'

'Yes, sir,' he replied with a smirk on his face.

As the burly corporal marched me towards the door, I glanced at Sergeant Smith from the corner of my eye to see him sigh with relief.

The following morning the orderly sergeant gave his version of events but obviously didn't mention anything about our conversation. I couldn't see any point in divulging it either; the way I saw it, I was in trouble whatever I said. After listening to the RSM's statement I knew mine was a lost cause.

Colonel Peck was a fair-minded man and had been very sympathetic with me when my father died, but on this occasion he was angry – very angry indeed. After a severe dressing down, I was sentenced to seven days' incarceration with loss of pay.

The lanky corporal seemed to derive great pleasure from the outcome, knowing full well I would be under his power for the next week. Apprehension and fear enveloped me as he marched aggressively towards me and brought one of his heavily studded boots crashing down about two inches from my feet, halting directly in front of me. His spittle literally splattered my face as he bellowed out orders. The sheer hostility in his voice shook me and an involuntary shiver ran down my spine, but despite his belligerent manner I somehow managed to keep my cool. I could tell by the snarl on his face that he sensed my fear and it was obvious that he gained pleasure from the power he held over me.

'Pick your feet up, you scumbag!' he shouted as I strutted across the camp towards the guardroom. 'I'll make a soldier out of you if it's the last thing I do!' He stalked my every movement, striving to incite fear in me with his constant bellowing.

On many occasions I'd seen him marching other prisoners at the double around the camp in the same aggressive manner and each time a shudder had run down my spine. Well, this time it was my turn to be on the receiving end of this savage creature's abuse. 'Don't let the bastard grind you down, John,' I thought. 'You've had to contend with bullies before.'

During my childhood I'd had to put up with many barbed comments in the schoolyard due to the fact that my dad was a rag-

and-bone man and had been to prison twice. Children can be very cruel and I certainly had to learn how to stick up for myself. Well, now I was a young man and a strong one at that, so I certainly wasn't going to let this harsh brute dampen my spirit. From that moment, I was determined to use his bullyboy tactics to my own advantage. I made it a challenge – it was him or me, and I certainly didn't intend to succumb easily. The strange thing is, I actually enjoyed the next seven days of confinement, but then I had help from above in the guise of Tommy Wilkins, my cellmate – and what a character he was.

_ 'Now get that uniform off!' bellowed the MP, throwing some grey denim pants and a shirt at me. 'And put these rags on!'

'This shirt's too big,' I complained, 'and it's moth-eaten.'

'Shut your mouth, you little shit!' he growled as he opened the cell door. 'Now get in there with that animal!'

This was my first meeting with Tommy, a rough-looking character with a stubbly beard. Tommy just put two fingers up to the corporal and grunted like a chimpanzee, baring his teeth.

'Bloomin' 'eck!' I thought as the MP slammed the door shut and turned the key. Who the heck's this and what have we got here?

The only natural light in the cell came from a small window in the steel door and a barred window fixed high into the outer wall and close to the ceiling. Other than the cell door we were enclosed within a 13-inch thick wall. The ambience of the cell appeared rather depressing, but Tommy soon changed all that.

He was 5 feet 7 inches tall, the same as me, and with a similar stocky frame, but other than that he was totally different, with a full shaven head like Yul Brynner and tattoos covering his arms, back and chest. My first impression was that he was coarse and unfriendly, but I was wrong. Underneath the bravado lay an affable, warmhearted, generous bloke with a mischievous sense of humour. We hit it off almost immediately and it soon became apparent he had a definite rebellious approach towards authority... especially this corporal.

Tommy didn't beat about the bush. 'What's your name and what are you in for then?'

'John,' I replied, and went on to tell him what had happened.

'So you're only in for a week, eh? A part-timer!'

'Aye, that's right... and you?'

'Just a month,' he replied casually.

'Bloody hell! A month!' I spluttered. 'That's a long time, in'it?'

'Ha ha ha! I could do that in my sleep. The last time I did three months.'

'Blimey! What did you do then?'

'I was fighting in the NAAFI Club near the docks and I laid out a couple of sailors. The military police got involved and it took four of 'em to arrest me and bring me in.'

'The MPs aren't very fond of you, I take it?'

'You can say that again, especially this dickhead of a corporal. I hate him!'

'I know what you mean. He's got a right callous streak, hasn't he?'

'He has that. He's notorious all right and he loves the reputation – he's a right sadistic bastard! I've seen many a man break down and cry because of his ways, but I personally wouldn't give him the satisfaction. Even when he's getting to me I just grin at him and it really goads him – I love it!'

'You know something? Similar thoughts went through my head as he was marching me over here, stomping his feet.'

'I hope you do stand up to him without flinching. It'd be great to have a bit o' back-up.'

'There's one thing for sure – I don't intend to bend to his will.'

'We'll see,' laughed Tommy. 'I've heard many a bloke say that but they always cracked!'

Tommy didn't mean to be intimidating – it was just his way. 'Listen, lad, I believe in getting to the point and calling a spade a spade. What's the use in pussyfooting about? He's a right bastard and you might as well know it from the word go.'

'Right, Tommy, I know what you mean. I've got to admit that he puts the wind up me, but I still intend to stick up to him.'

'Good for you. Like I said, we'll see… Anyway, it'll be good to watch.'

'We *will* see,' I thought to myself. 'I'm determined not to let that barbaric thug break my spirit.' I didn't either, but those seven days tested my willpower to the limit.

'Hang on a minute – that'll be the pig now,' said Tommy, as a key turned in the cell door. 'He's probably coming back for you, 'cos he enjoys putting prisoners through their paces on their first day in nick.'

'Right, you measly excuse for a man!' the MP rapped as he glanced into the cell. 'Out here now at the double – and put that on!' he hissed, pointing to a large rucksack kitted out with full battle gear.

'Blimey!' I thought, as I hitched it to my back. 'This must be loaded with stones – it weighs a ton.'

The corporal sniggered, knowing full well the rucksack was weighted down.

'Now get your arse outside, you friggin' little gobshite, and stand to attention till I'm ready for you!'

After I'd stood for an hour, he marched me across to a large playing field directly facing the guardroom and ordered me to run round its perimeter until he told me to stop. By the time I'd run around it twice I was dripping wet as sweat poured from me. Now it was dinnertime and some of my mates waved encouragingly at me as they made their way to the mess hall.

The MP didn't like the attention I was getting, so he took over again. 'Quick march, quick march, you scumbag!' he bawled, marching me back to the brig at the double. 'That'll do for starters,' he snarled, shoving me back into the cell, slamming to the steel door shut. 'Now get back in your rat hole where you belong – with that other maggot!'

'How did you get on?' smirked Tommy, sprawled out on the bed with his arms behind his head.

'To tell the truth, I enjoyed it. I got a rush of adrenaline out there. Anyway, it was better than being cooped up in this dingy place.' Unbeknown to the corporal, I'd built myself into prime condition since entering the Army and I thrived on physical exercise.

'That's good, because making prisoners run around that field is his favourite punishment. It really gets to most blokes.'

'Well, it won't get to me,' I laughed. 'I could put up with that all day. Anyroad, doesn't he make you do it?'

'Does he bloody hell! He's given up on me!' He roared laughing.

A few minutes later the cell door opened again and the corporal entered, carrying a tray containing two dinners. He handed one to Tommy and then turned to me.

'Get this down your throat and be quick about it!' he snarled. 'And don't get yourself settled because I'll be back shortly. There'll be loads o' washing up to do afterwards.'

Sure enough, ten minutes later he returned and stood there arrogantly with a self-satisfied look on his face, thinking he'd got one over on me. 'On your feet, you little gobshite! Out here now and bring them bloody plates with you!'

Bloomin' 'eck! I thought. Hasn't he got a polite word in his vocabulary at all?

Outside the cell, in the main body of the guardroom, were six beds where the soldiers on guard duty slept, and a small office to accommodate the MPs. At the back of the room were two toilets and a small kitchen.

'Right, you moron, you can wash that lot as well,' he snarled, pointing to a pile of dinner plates, mugs and cutlery on a wooden table. 'And you'd better not break anything!'

After I'd finished he ordered me to carry everything back to the mess hall at the far end of the camp, and then scrub a large stone floor on my hands and knees.

That night the atmosphere was much better because the MP finished at 1800 hours and ordinary soldiers took over until 0600. Tommy was in a giddy mood and wanted to lark about.

'Come on, John, let's have a wrestle! I've got a load of energy I want to get rid of.'

'No way! It's all right for you – you've been lounging about on your bed all day. I'm knackered. And anyroad, I want to build up some energy to impress our friendly MP tomorrow.'

But he wouldn't have it and jumped on me trying to get me into a headlock. Nevertheless, I was too slithery and soon we were grappling on the floor, all in good fun. He was very strong, but so was I. As we rolled about the floor, I could feel his aggressiveness and thanked God I'd kept fit, making us well matched.

'E-eh, I enjoyed that,' he gasped after about ten minutes. 'That was great!'

After a short respite he began to feel energetic again.

'Watch this, John,' he laughed, 'I'll bet you can't do this.' The next minute he started to walk on his hands but soon tumbled to the floor.

'That's easy,' I said, 'and I know why you fell over. You're doing it wrong.'

'Oh aye, clever sod? Let's see *you* do it then.'

To his amazement I stood on my hands and walked the length of the room, turned around and walked back again.

'There, what did I tell you?' I smirked, feeling cocky.

'Bloody hell! I've always wanted to do it like that! Come on, show me how it's done?'

'Sure, you've almost got the knack of it. The trouble is, you're not taking your legs far enough forward in front of your head and that's why you lose your balance.'

'Go on then, show me!' he blurted excitedly.

'Right,' I asked after going into a handstand, 'can you see how far forward my feet are past my head?'

'Yeah I can, but how come you don't fall over onto your back then?'

'Well, it's something that you've got to get a feel for. If I'm going to topple over, I just adjust my hands forward accordingly. I'll tell you what – I'll do it again, but this time you take notice of what I've been saying.'

He watched me excitedly as I pranced about the cell. 'Right, I'm with you. Now get out of the way and let me have a go!'

He struggled at first but with perseverance he mastered it and once he got the idea there was no stopping him. It was hilarious to see him walking around the guardroom on his hands, giggling like a young schoolboy. I felt I had made a friend for life.

'Watch me, John – this should get a laugh,' he said, knocking on the cell door, requesting to go to the toilet. By the time the door opened, Tommy was ready and to the amusement of the guardroom soldiers, he walked past them on his hands all the way to and from the toilet, leaving them all in stitches.

'That was great!' he laughed when he returned to the cell. 'They wondered what the bloody hell was going on – I love it, I love it!'

'I've got to give it to you, Tommy,' I mused. 'You've certainly got the hang of it now. That was a superb performance.'

'Yeah, it was, wasn't it – thanks to you, John. Anyway, how about another bout of wrestling? I'm feeling energetic.'

'Oh, come off it, Tommy! Give us a break after what our friend put me through today.'

He just cracked out laughing. 'All right, don't have a heart attack – I'm only kidding!'

'Thank goodness for that!' I thought, settling down for a good night's kip.

Next morning after a sparse breakfast the RSM did an inspection accompanied by the smug corporal.

To my surprise the RSM asked me, 'Any complaints, Private Cowell?'

'No, sir. Thank you, sir.'

'Bloomin' 'eck, Tommy!' I said afterwards. 'How come he asked me that? Am I in favour or what?'

'No way! It's obligatory.'

'How d'you mean?'

'Well, it's laid down in the rulebook. He has to ask every prisoner that question, and you know what a stickler the RSM is for following the rules.'

'D'you mean to say he'll ask me that question every morning?'

'That's right, and not only that – he has to take any complaint seriously and follow it up.'

'U-um, that's handy to know… very handy indeed.'

My newfound knowledge was soon put to the test after I'd knocked on the cell door requesting some toothpaste, only to be greeted by the corporal.

'Oh, you haven't any toothpaste have you not, you scruffy little urchin!' he snarled sarcastically. 'Well, you'll just have to scrub your teeth with soap, won't you!'

'No, corporal, I can't do that. I want some toothpaste, please.'

'Well, you're not bloody well getting any! Understand?'

'If you don't get me any then I'm afraid I'll have to report the matter to the RSM in the morning.'

'What did you say, soldier?' he spat, nearly swallowing his tongue.

'I'll have to report...'

'Shut your mouth, you lippy, bickering worm and get your arse out here and put that on!' he fumed, pointing to the full battledress. 'You think you had it hard the other day? Well, now I'm really going to put you through your paces!'

Once again he had me running around the playing field, and just like before the sweat oozed from every pore of my body. At one point I felt downtrodden but then I thought of Tommy and it spurred me on.

After the fourth time around he stopped me and growled, 'Now do you feel like changing your mind?'

There was no chance, as I was now beginning to enjoy it. Other soldiers had yielded under this treatment but most of them were smokers, whereas I'd never touched a cigarette in my life.

'No, Corporal,' I replied, defiantly looking him straight in the eyes. 'I still want some toothpaste.' I knew he was ruffled because I noticed nerves twitching in his face.

'Are you taking the piss, you mangy git?' he cursed, along with a few more choice words.

I said nothing but just stood there staring defiantly back at him. His frustration built up even more and little red blood vessels appeared to erupt in his eyes as he towered above me. He snorted through his nose as he summoned up more venom from within his bulky frame, and his arms tightened up like steel as he clenched his fists.

His very presence intimidated my whole being, but somehow I managed to hold steadfast. 'Stand your ground, John lad,' I said to myself. 'Don't let this coward of a man grind you down.'

My tactics seemed to be working – he began to look unsure of himself. For lack of anything better to say he screeched, 'Right, you little scumbag! Go on, get running until I tell you to stop – at the double!'

As I ran around the field I came to the notice of some off-duty soldiers and they all started to cheer, encouraging me to plod on in the same way my mates had done previously. There was no need, as once I got my second wind I felt I could go on indefinitely. By now the corporal was panicking somewhat, frightened that I might collapse or something.

'Have you had enough yet, you little bastard?' he grunted, frothing at the mouth.

'No, Corporal,' I smirked, once again looking him right in the eyes. 'I'm enjoying this. Can I go round again?'

'No, you bloody well can't!' he yelled, resentment showing in his face. 'Get yourself over to the guardroom – now!'

When I got into the cell I collapsed on my bed, absolutely exhausted.

'Good lad,' said Tommy. 'Well done! I watched you from the cell window by pulling myself up on the bars. That pig of a corporal was bloody fuming! Great!'

I didn't get any more aggravation from the corporal that day and the following morning when he did his rounds with the RSM he looked rather passive.

'Right, Private Cowell,' asked the RSM, 'have you any complaints?'

I purposely pondered for a moment, first looking at the corporal, before replying, 'No, sir. Thank you, sir.'

The MP sighed with relief and it clearly showed on his face. After that he relented a bit towards me – he must have thought I was another Tommy – but I still didn't get any toothpaste.

The friendship with Tommy made the time spent in the cell more bearable, especially when something happened that I found hilarious.

Tommy was lovesick, having a girlfriend in Plymouth who hadn't visited him since being locked up. 'I've tried writing to her but I'm bloody hopeless with letters. I haven't got a clue where to start; I'm no good at words.'

'Just put down what you feel about her,' I said, as though I was the expert. 'Girls like to hear nice things, you know.'

'Hey, hang on a minute. You seem to know a bit about it – you write a letter for me!'

'Get lost, Tommy! I can't do that. Anyroad, she'd know in a crack that it wasn't your handwriting.'

'All right then – just say anything that comes into your head and I'll scribble it down.'

'Aye, go on then. Anything for a bit of piece and quiet,' I replied, feeling a bit mischievous. So I scribbled something like this on a piece of paper:

'My dearest darling Helena, with all my heart I'd like to express my undying love for you but my imagination cannot capture the reality of your being. Your beauty is far beyond words or pen, the elegance of the sun, the stars or anything in the entire universe, and my feeling for you goes far deeper than the deepest ocean. The flowers, the trees, the birds – everything that is beautiful reminds me of you…' And so on in this vein.

I was only joking but he copied everything I'd jotted down, more or less word for word. I couldn't believe it next morning when he told me he'd posted the letter.

'You haven't written down what I said, have you, Tommy?'

'Too true I have. It brought tears to my eyes before I sealed it up. If that doesn't do the trick, I don't know what will!'

'Crikey!' I cringed inwardly as I scratched my head. 'I hope so. Tommy, I really do.'

Well, nobody was more surprised than me by what happened next. Helena received the letter and it worked a treat. The following evening she came to visit him and the meeting was all lovey-dovey and kissy-kissy.

'Thanks, mate,' Tommy smirked after Helena had left. 'That was great – I owe you one. She's well in love with me again.' For the remainder of that night he was happy as a lark.

The remaining days in the cooler passed quickly and although I didn't relish being locked up, my time there was very memorable – but I was still glad to be released.

I was thinking of Tommy when the sound of familiar orders brought me back to reality, back on the *Devonshire*.

'Quick march! On the double! Left right, left right, you miserable critters!'

U-um, I thought as I watched the two MPs marching the two soldiers around the deck. They can't be any more sadistic than that swine of a corporal back in Plymouth...

'Hey John,' said big Bri one morning, 'd'you fancy pairing up with me in a competition of deck bowling?'

'*Deck* bowling? How can you play bowls on a ship? The flamin' balls will run all o'er the place!'

'They don't play with bowls, you silly sod! They use hoops made from rope, which you slide along the deck towards a bull's-eye.'

'Yeah, righto – I'll have a go at that.'

Like Bri said, the game – called quoits – involved sliding rope rings along the deck, about the length of a cricket pitch, towards a large circular target with some outer rings. The bull scored 50 and the outer rings scored 30, 20 and 10 respectively. The game must have been invented for Brian and me because we sailed through the early rounds and reached the final without conceding a leg, but we didn't have it all our own way in the final.

All previous heats had been the best of three legs but the final was the best of 5. The deck was swarming with supporters, mainly for the two other finalists, who were infantrymen. Nevertheless when Bri and I entered the arena we also got a good reception. 'Come on, big Bri! Come on, John! Show 'em what the medics can do,' shouted our mates.

Brian and I felt confident and after a few practice shots my bosom buddy said, 'Right, John – I'm as ready as I'll ever be. How about you?'

'Yeah, Bri – let's go! We can only do our best.'

The other two lads were highly competitive and took the first leg, winning 21-16. Brian and I dug deep and something must have stirred, because after that we ran away with the game, winning the next three legs by 21-9, 21-14 and 21-11.

Cheers resounded around the deck as we received our trophies and £4 each. The runners-up were good sports too and congratulated us, saying we'd played well and were worthy winners.

Sailing past the mouth of the Mediterranean we spotted the African coastline but it was just a haze in the far distance. Later, however, we passed a group of islands which were much closer.

'Land ahoy on the port side!' shouted one of the soldiers.

'Hey, look at those islands over there!' shouted others excitedly.

'D'you know what they call 'em, John?' asked Rob, edging to the rail for a closer look.

'Do I 'eck as like! I haven't a clue, Rob – do you?'

'Yeah, they're the Canaries.'

'What, do you mean the Canary Islands?'

'I sure do – you've got it in one!'

'Bloomin' 'eck, Rob! I wish we were going there instead of the Cameroons.'

'Aye, so do I. It'd be great, wouldn't it? I've heard that the young Spanish women are absolutely gorgeous. Cor! The very thought of kipping up with one of them beauties makes me feel like diving in and swimming over there.'

'In your dreams,' I laughed. 'Still, there might be some beauties in the Cameroons.'

'Aye, you never know… I hope you're right.' He giggled like a young schoolboy and then asked me, 'Anyway John, while we're on about the Canaries – why do you think they call them the Canary Islands?'

'Oh, I think that's easy – it's probably because the islands are full of canaries.'

'Well, you think wrong. In fact, it was the other way round – the birds got their name from the islands.'

'What are you talking about? I don't get it.'

'No, I didn't think you would.'

'All right, know it all – are you going to tell me or what?'

'Well, what it is… Canary Islands literally translates as Island of Dogs.'

'Dogs! How can it mean dogs?'

'Right, I'll tell you a little history. I suppose you've heard about Christopher Columbus?'

'Yeah, he's the fellow who discovered America, isn't he?'

'That's right, but before that he discovered these islands. When the Spanish began to colonise them, they discovered that the islands were full of dogs. There were many different species and some were transported back to Spain to be bred and trained on the King's estate.'

'U-um, that's interesting, but it still doesn't explain why they called them the Canary Islands.'

'Ah well, that's the clever bit,' gloated Rob. 'It's because the word "canary" derives from the word "canine", which means doglike.'

'Oh, that is clever. I like it... it all fits together like a jigsaw puzzle. That's a little bit more useless information I can add to my list of knowledge,' I laughed.

The islands gradually faded into the far distance until they were no more than a blob on the horizon. It certainly was a special time and I felt really good inside. The entire crew took on a happy mood as we gazed across the crystal-clear ocean and our joy became even more apparent as many dolphins joined in the fun, and this time hundreds of flying fish swam alongside them. Once again I was enthralled by the playful antics of the dolphins as they dived and frolicked near the bow of the ship, missing it by inches as it ploughed steadily through the water. I later learned that the waters surrounding the Canary Islands were ideal breeding grounds for dolphins due to their depth and various species of marine life.

My geography and nautical terms were improving by this stage of the voyage. From my limited knowledge I already knew that America lay to the west of England and that the sun rose from the east. Every day I noticed that the sun rose from the left side of the ship over Africa, and every night it set on the right side over the large expanse of the Atlantic Ocean. I was aware that the ship was heading south and this got me thinking.

'U-um, let me see,' I pondered out loud. 'Japan is the land of the rising sun in the Far East so it must lie over there beyond Africa, and as the sun always sets in the west, America must be over there to the right side of the boat.'

'What are you thinking about, John?' asked Johnny Walker, a Liverpudlian who'd served 5 years in the Merchant Navy.

When I told him what I'd concluded he laughed a little. 'You're on the right track but as you're on a ship, why don't you use the proper terms?'

'How d'you mean, Johnny?'

'Well, for a start, you shouldn't say left or right side of a ship – you should use the terms "port" and "starboard".'

'And which is which?'

'The port side is always on the left when facing the nose or bow of the ship, and the starboard is always on the right.'

'That's all very well, but how the hell do I remember which is which?'

'Ah, good question. I'm not too sure where the name port side comes from – maybe it's because passengers always board ships on that side. However, I'm dead sure about starboard: it translates to "steering side" because centuries ago small boats were steered by a paddle that hung over the right side of the vessel. So if you get mixed up by which is which, just think that you're steering a boat by paddling on the right side and you'll know that's the starboard side. Got it?'

'Yeah, thanks Johnny – that's a really good way of explaining it. All I have to remember now is which side of the small boats the paddle was on and I've cracked it.'

'Go on, you daft bugger!'

'Joking aside, that was a good tale. I'll remember that.'

I did too. I seemed to be acquiring quite a bit of knowledge from my shipmates.

Further down the African coast the ship had to drop anchor in a bay at Dakar, the capital of Senegal, to take on supplies and top up our water.

Scores of local natives, mostly young boys, sailed out to greet us in small boats and started to dive into the deep water to retrieve the pennies that the soldiers were throwing overboard.

Others, carrying trinkets and oddments carved from wood, started to barter with the troops to sell their wares. I couldn't make out some of the items from the deck but I noticed a lot of lads negotiating with the natives through the portholes of our sleeping quarters, which were closer to the water. Many of the young boys held up long poles displaying their wares, but kept them just out of reach of the soldiers. Some of the troops, in devilment, pretended they needed a closer look at the object and then tried to snatch it. But the natives were too canny and kept it just out of arm's reach. Wanting in on the action, I rushed down to the lower deck and went into haggling mode.

'You like this?' asked a young boy, holding up a sculpture of an elephant beautifully carved out of dark wood. 'You give me three shillings... I give you elephant.'

'No, three shillings is too much... I give two shillings,' I answered in the same Pidgin English.

'No no, three shillings is very good price... elephant take much time to make.'

'Yes, but I'm not a rich man. I give you two shillings... no more.'

'All right, sir... because you are my friend I do good deal.'

'Oh yeah,' I laughed. 'I'll bet you've got a lot of friends!'

'Catch!' he said, throwing me a piece of string.

'What's this for?' I asked.

'You hold one end... I tie other end to elephant and you pull.'

'Oh, I see. But what about the two shillings... I throw, you catch?'

'Ha ha ha! You throw in water... I dive for it.'

'But you might lose it.'

'I no lose... you throw, I find.' He did too, laughing loudly as he emerged from the deep water clutching the two-shilling piece in his hand.

It was great to watch the boys as they retrieved the coins effortlessly from the deep-sea water. I used to like diving into the local swimming pool back home to retrieve pennies, but that was nothing compared to this.

They were a friendly bunch all right. After salvaging more coins the young man started to chat with me again and after asking my name, he came out with an expression I'd never heard before.

'You like jig-a-jig, Mr John?'

'Jig-a-jig... what is jig-a-jig?' I asked, nonplussed.

'Jig-a-jig! You know, Mr John... with the ladies,' he giggled, grinning from ear to ear.

'Oh, I see... that's what you call it in this part of the world, is it?'

He grinned all the more. 'Yes! If you like, Mr John, I find much ladies for you... you have plenty good time, yes?'

'Sounds good,' I replied. 'Also not so good, because we're not allowed to leave the ship till we reach the Cameroons.'

'That is very long way... Cameroon ladies no good jig-a-jig like Dakar. I come for you tonight in boat and take you to very nice lady... you have plenty good time, yes?'

'You must be joking!' I laughed. 'I'd be clapped in irons and they'd throw away the key, but thanks all the same.'

'Goodbye, Mr John,' he said, moving towards another porthole to sell more merchandise.

We'd been anchored for about two hours when something extraordinary happened. French planes flew over our ship and dropped hundreds of paratroopers. At first they looked like flies in the sky, but as they got lower we could make out definite shapes of parachutes. They all glided systematically inland, presumably landing at their base camp. The display must have been put on for our benefit, because it seemed too coincidental that it took place just as we happened to be docking there. I often wondered if our government had arranged it with the French – I don't think so, but you never know.

It was a nice demonstration and good to watch but another exhibition a few moments later got us much more interested and excited. A small French passenger ship carrying lots of young women pulled in and dropped anchor on our port side. The decks of the ship were lit up like the Blackpool illuminations, and flocks of onlookers showed their interest by cheering and waving at us. This created interest throughout our ship and got lots of the troops excited. We exchanged greetings with them by waving our shirts about and shouting messages. The intensity built up when some mischievous young women started to wave back with articles of underwear. They were teasing us, knowing full well we couldn't do a thing about it even if we wanted to. All the same, we enjoyed the fun and it gave us something to laugh and joke about – it certainly boosted morale. These friendly exchanges took place right up to the moment of our departure, when something very special happened.

As our ship's engines roared into action, our lads again started to sing 'Now is the Hour'. Just as at Southampton, a silence descended upon our ship and transmitted itself to the French boat. At that moment I got an indescribable tingling from the top of my head to the tip of my toes, and I felt that all the troops and the passengers on the French boat were experiencing the same emotions as me. It is a memory that I will always cherish.

That night the lads talked about the paratroopers but the main topic of conversation centred on the French ladies waving their knickers and, of course, jig-a-jig.

'You like jig-a-jig, I give you plenty jig-a-jig,' lots of the men kept repeating, full of zest.

'I can't wait to get off this ship,' said one of the lads. 'I'm rampant... let me get at 'em!'

'Aye, me too,' said another. 'Jig-a-jig here I come!'

The subject of jig-a-jig was at the forefront of everybody's mind, including mine, and the matter soon came to the attention of the commanding officer. Next morning he called us all to the deck and we got a lecture from a medical officer.

'Right, gentlemen. I know you are all under the impression that the women in the Cameroons are free and easy, and this may be the case, but I must make you aware of the dangers. Venereal disease and gonorrhoea are rife in this part of the world and if you have sexual intercourse with anyone at all you will be putting yourself at serious risk. The strain of gonorrhoea in this part of Africa is very hard to cure as it is resistant to the usual types of drugs we use to combat the disease, and if anyone contracts it there is a serious danger of it turning to syphilis. Another thing: any soldier who becomes infected is liable to be put on a charge.'

'That's put me off,' I said after the lecture. 'I'm going to keep myself to myself till I get back home to dear old Blighty.'

'Yeah, me too,' said Jimmy. 'I don't fancy catching a dose... u-ugh!'

'Go on, you soft buggers,' said one of the regular soldiers. 'Don't let a bit o' scaremongering put you off! They give that same bloody lecture every time a troopship docks, no matter which bloody country it is.'

'That may be so,' I said, 'but it's still put me off.'

'Well, it's not going to put me off, that's for sure,' sniggered another lad.

'No, me neither,' echoed a few others.

We left it at that but later in the dining room Brian spluttered, 'U-ugh! This tea tastes bloody awful!'

'Do you know something, lads?' said Rob. 'The bloody swines have gone and put bromide in the tea.'

'Bromide? What's bromide?' asked one rather naive lad.

'Bromide is something to stop you feeling randy,' laughed Jimmy and Brian. 'The CO's trying to put a stop to our antics before we even get started.'

'Antics – is that another name for jig-a-jig?' joked Rob, rolling about in laughter.

'All right, I only asked,' said the poor lad. 'No need to take the piss.'

This of course only made the lads laugh even more…

The days passed and eventually the coastline of the Cameroons appeared on the horizon with a snowcapped mountain in the background.

'Just look at that, Rob,' I said feeling awed. 'It's fantastic, in'it?'

'You'll not think so after you've patrolled it a few times,' quipped Rob. 'I'm wondering what sort of a place they've brought us to. It looks an ideal habitat for guerillas.'

'Trust you to think of that! Don't get me going – I haven't had the jitters since leaving Blighty.'

Finally we dropped anchor half a mile offshore at Victoria in the

British Cameroons. As at Dakar, scores of small boats sailed out to greet us. It was still forbidden to leave the ship, but this time lots of lads ignored the order and dived into the deep blue seawater.

'Bloomin' 'eck Rob!' I said. 'That water looks cool and inviting, doesn't it?'

'You're not thinking o' joining 'em, are you, John? You'll be thrown into the brig quicker than you can blink if you're caught.'

'I am that. I'm sure the CO's turning a blind eye, 'cos the deck sergeant must have spotted them lads by now.'

'On your own head be it... I know I wouldn't risk it.'

I knew he was talking sense but as I looked down at the other lads splashing about in the cool water, the temptation was too great. I just couldn't resist it and dived in among them.

A few lads climbed aboard some of the natives' boats and exchanged greetings. Laughter soon broke out as the conversation once again focused on jig-a-jig.

'You like good jig-a-jig?' asked one young boy. 'I get you plenty!'

'Young ladies?' asked one of the soldiers.

'Yes, very young, very pretty and plenty good jig-a-jig... I get for you!'

'Oh yeah, and what's the catch?'

'Catch... what is "catch"?' asked the young boy. 'I no understand.'

'What I mean is, do we have to pay?'

'Oh yes, you pay, but only 5 shillings.'

'Five shillings! That's too much!'

'No, no, is very cheap... my sister give you plenty good time.'

'Your *sister!*' spluttered the soldier, nearly falling out of the boat.

'Yes, my sister, she very pretty,' replied the young boy, puzzled as to why the soldier had reacted in such a manner. To him it seemed as normal as us eating fish and chips back home.

Our conversation was interrupted by Rob shouting down from the deck. 'You'd best get yourselves back up here as quick as you can! There's gonna be a deck inspection in 20 minutes.'

Along with the others I swam for the ship and started to clamber up the anchor chain. The thick, heavy chain ran from the main deck through a two-foot diameter steel funnel in the body of the ship.

'Bloody hell!' I thought as I made my way from one huge steel link to another and through the funnel. 'I must be crazy doing this – if the ship moves, I'll be crushed like a fly.' Was I glad to reach the deck safely! Luckily, we got away scot-free with our little misdemeanour.

After tea we were summoned to the large hall.

'Come on, you scruffy lot!' bellowed the RSM. 'This is your last night aboard this ship. Playtime's over – as from tomorrow you're going to find out what Army life is really about. Settle down now and take heed – the CO wants to address you. Attention!'

'Right, gentlemen, at ease!' ordered the Commanding Officer. 'Like the RSM said, life from tomorrow is going to be very different. You've had it nice and easy during our pleasant voyage but things won't be quite so relaxed once we leave the ship. You're soldiers, and I expect you to act like soldiers. Just remember everything that you've been taught in training and work together as a team – a happy squad makes for a proficient squad.

'Once we reach the mainland we will be splitting up to form three camps. The main camp will be set up in Buea, which is about 20 miles up the coast, where the bulk of you will be stationed. The second camp is in Kumba, 50 miles inland in thick jungle territory, and 120 troops will be posted there, with attachments from the Medics, the Signals, the REME and the Service Corps. The third camp is in Bamenda, over 200 miles from here up in the mountains and I'll be sending many infantrymen there, also with attachments.

'The whereabouts of the each camp has been kept from you for security reasons, but as from now you will find a mandate on the noticeboard informing each and every one of you of your postings. Finally, gentlemen, I'd just like to add… good luck to you all!'

We were all curious to know where we were going and couldn't wait to look at the orders.

'Bloomin' 'eck!' I groaned. 'I'm going to Kumba, right in the thick of the jungle… Is anybody else going there?'

'Not me,' said Brian. 'I'm going to Buea.'

'Me too,' said Jimmy Mitchinson.

'What about you, Nev?'

'No, I'm going to Bamenda, up in the mountains,' he replied.

'Crikey! Is nobody going to Kumba?' I asked, feeling edgy.

'I am,' said Rob.

'Great!' I said. 'At least I'll know somebody then. What about Ted?'

'Ted's going to Bamenda with me,' answered Neville.

It didn't turn out as bad as I'd feared, because seven other medics from our squad were heading for Kumba as well. Also, Martin Grogan was going to the same posting, albeit in the infantry. I felt sad about Jimmy and big Bri going to Buea – they were a good mates and I knew I'd miss them.

'Ah well, at least that's sorted,' said Bri. 'We may as well meet up tonight in the bar for a last-night piss up – what do you say?'

'Yeah, fair enough,' everybody agreed.

'Until then I'm gonna laze around and soak up the sun,' announced big Bri. 'It may be the last chance we get.'

I joined him for a short while, but then spent the rest of the day playing deck quoits with Jimmy. Later that evening, before joining the lads, I walked about the deck, taking in the beauty of the night. A beautiful red sky contrasted with the clear waters against the backdrop of a tree-covered coastline with mountains beyond. Many natives were still bartering with soldiers, while others fished and lazed about in boats nearer to the shore. The silhouette of the little boats added to the beauty and peace all around. Everything appeared so alluring, tranquil and untroubled.

'It's funny,' I thought. 'Everything about this place seems to be at one with nature, yet we're out here to sort out an uprising.'

I then said a little prayer: 'Please God, keep close to me and my friends in this Third World country and protect us from harm. May I always see the world as I see it at this moment. And finally, please keep watch over all my family back home. Thank you, God, amen!'

Big Bri interrupted my little invocation: 'John, are you coming or what?'

'Yeah, all right. I'll be with you in a minute.'

'What's up, John? You seem to be miles away.'

'Sorry, Bri – I was just reminiscing and admiring the sunset. Just look at it… it's absolutely stunning.'

'Maybe it is, but we've got months to admire it while we're stuck out here in this Godforsaken country. Come on, let's go for a drink with the other lads to celebrate our last night together for a while.'

Godforsaken? I thought. How can he say that with all this beauty around?

Nonetheless, I did agree that this was a night to celebrate. I'd had the time of my life on this voyage and didn't want to leave the *Devonshire*. But all good things come to an end and this would be the last time we would all be together, so I picked up speed and followed Brian to where the lads were having a singalong and a drinking session. The overall mood was melancholy, as for many of us it was the parting of the ways. It was sad because we'd grown towards each other like a family and didn't know if we'd ever see each other again.

Also it was the end of our summer vacation… we now had to face the dangers of what our time in Africa had in store for us and the uncertainty of what lay ahead.

CHAPTER FOUR

THE BRITISH
CAMEROONS – KUMBA

'Come on, you lazy lot!' shouted Spud Murphy. 'Time to get up! The holiday's over… we've got some real soldiering to do now!'

Butterflies built up in my stomach again as the truth started to dawn on me. The fact that we were going to a war-torn state had been suppressed during the enjoyable voyage, but at this moment stark reality stared me straight in the face. My fear intensified as news filtered through that a soldier from the Royal Engineers in an advance party had been killed. Rumours had it that his truck had run off the road into a deep basin… I never did find out what really happened but it occurred to me that in this kind of situation, it was inevitable that more of us would be killed. Once again I imagined hundreds of African warriors charging at us and wielding machetes.

'Stop it, John! Get a grip on yourself!' I muttered to myself as I emptied my bedside locker and stuffed the contents into my kitbag. I left the confined sleeping quarters with a tinge of sadness, which struck me as strange, given the way I felt when I first set eyes on the place.

'Come on, John,' said Brian. 'We'd best make our way up to the main deck.'

'Yeah, righto, Bri. Just give me a minute.'

Before I followed the others I knelt down and said my final prayer before leaving the ship:

'Please God, protect me and my comrades during our mission in the Cameroons and keep us safe from harm. I don't want to do any wrong to my fellow man even though he be my enemy, so please be with us at all times and grant us the wisdom to do the right thing under difficult circumstances, should the need arise.'

'Say one for me, John,' said a couple of men, tapping me on the shoulder as they passed.

'I have done, lads – don't worry about it,' I replied, rising from my knees.

The deck was a hive of activity as corporals and sergeants issued orders. Then the CO's voice came over the loud speaker: 'Attention, everybody! All soldiers going to Kumba and Bamenda must assemble in the entertainment hall until further notice. All those going to Buea, remain on deck and prepare for disembarkation. We leave within the hour.'

Before they marched off I bade goodbye to my friends, especially big Brian and Jimmy.

The lads going to Bamenda vacated the ship next and finally at 1400 hours came our turn. After making our way down steps at the side of the ship, we boarded landing boats, which carried us towards the shore. The jungle came right up to the shoreline and the dock was just an old broken-down jetty. How nobody got hurt climbing up an old rickety ladder onto the rotting pier is beyond belief. We found it very difficult trying to negotiate broken timbers while carrying full battle gear. To make matters worse, the jetty was covered in slimy moss, making it very slippery. Anyone overbalancing would have crashed into rocky waters 15 feet below and could have been badly injured.

Several three-ton Bedford trucks were parked ready to take us to Kumba. The other medics accompanying Rob and me were Maurice Sutcliffe, Mark Radiven, Peter Jenkins, Bill Hubhoard, Rodney Marsh and Spud Murphy, and we were attached to B Company.

'Fifty miles to go – we should get there in about an hour,' said Bill.

'What time is it now?' asked Rob.

'Five o'clock,' replied Pete, 'so according to Bill's reckoning we should reach camp about six o'clock.'

That's what we thought but we hadn't taken into account the state of the road – and it was the monsoon season. It wasn't a road at all, more a dirt trail, and following heavy rainfalls it was more like a muddy tank track. As we passed through little hamlets, many natives came out of their tiny mud huts and waved at us, expressing their delight to see us with big smiling faces. Halfway into the journey one of the rear trucks got bogged down and it was all hands to the pumps. Unfortunately it was becoming dark and the only light given off was from fireflies. It was nine o'clock before we reached Kumba, sludged up to the eyeballs.

The campsite was in a jungle clearing and the climate was hot, sticky and clammy. Two soldiers, both with rifles over their shoulders, patrolled the gate within yards of the guardroom while another stood to attention at the foot of a long flagpole, which was flying the Union Jack. A corporal marched from the guardroom to greet us but wouldn't allow us to enter the camp until he'd thoroughly examined our papers, scrutinising every document.

Weeks previously an advance party of Royal Engineers had built some Australian bush huts, housing between 30 and 40 men. The medics' hut, however, was much smaller with only eight beds. The huts, all open-plan, were constructed of corrugated tin sheets on a concrete base. We were all looking forward to a wash and brush-up after our arduous journey, but no such luck. Maybe the high-ranking officers had warm running water at their disposal, but for us privates there was no chance.

'If you want a wash there's a large water tank at the other side of camp near the latrines, where you can fill a bucket,' said one of the engineers.

'*What*? D'you mean we've got to wash in cold water?' I asked.

'That's right,' laughed a sergeant. 'Until we get this camp up and running that's the best thing on offer!'

'Bloody hell!' said Bill. 'I'm caked in mud... how the flamin' 'eck am I supposed to get this lot off?'

'Like I said, you'll have to…'

'I know, don't remind me… I'll have to wash in cold water.'

'Yes,' said the sergeant, 'and don't forget there'll be an inspection parade in the morning so you'll have to turn out presentable.'

'Inspection parade? You must be joking!' said Bill.

'It's no joke. You know the rules; this is what you've been trained for.'

Just then, much to our delight, we heard the bugler playing, 'Come to the Cookhouse Door, Boys.'

'Great!' I thought. 'Time for something to eat – I'm starving.'

On our way over we had to jump from duckboard to duckboard to avoid sinking into the deep mud, but even so some of it still squelched through the battens.

The canteen was constructed in a similar way to the other huts but was much larger and built onto the end was the divisional headquarters, housing the Commanding Officer and other high-ranking officers. The dining area served a double purpose as in between mealtimes it became the NAAFI Club where the written orders were listed daily. After feeding our faces, my mate Pete and I browsed through them, hoping we wouldn't be on guard duty. To my delight I wasn't, but I did have another task to perform.

'Look at this, Pete,' I said. 'I'm on Paludrine duty in the morning.'

'How do you mean – *Paludrine* duty?'

'Well, according to this, I've got to walk alongside the RSM in the morning during inspection parade and make sure every soldier takes a Paludrine tablet to prevent malaria.'

'Hey, that's a cushy number in'it? I hope I get to do it.'

'Don't worry, you will,' said a rather effeminate voice from behind us.

We turned round to see a sergeant in his mid-thirties, sporting a medics cap badge.

'Hello, boys,' he said with an alluring smile. 'Pleased to meet you. I'm the sergeant in charge of the medics.'

'Oh, right, Sarge,' I stammered, standing to attention. 'I'm John Cowell and this is Pete Jenkins.'

'No need for that, you can stand at ease. I won't bite,' he said in his camp manner. He weighed us up and down for a moment before saying, 'Anyway, I'll see you both tomorrow morning in the hospital directly after inspection parade. Goodnight, sleep tight, the pair of you.'

'Blimey!' stuttered Pete when the sergeant had gone. 'Where the bloody hell did they dig *her* up from? It looks like we've got a matron in charge of us!'

I tried to play down the situation because my dad always told me, 'If you can't say anything nice about a person, our John, then it's best to say nothing at all.'

'Don't be like that, Pete,' I said. 'At least she means well and seems to be thoughtful and caring.'

'*She* means well, does she? Oo-ohh, you could be right there.'

I couldn't believe what I'd just said but I certainly hadn't said it with malice or forethought. It just came out naturally after hearing Pete refer to him in that manner. This was only the start; I'd set a precedent for things to come.

Afterwards we made our way to the ablutions, where loads of blokes stood stark naked, washing their muddy clothes before swilling themselves down. The engineers had constructed some shower units made up of bamboo partitions but they were not yet up and running. Alongside them was a line of similar tiny cubicles which housed the toilets but they weren't what you could call The Ritz. A long deep ditch, which was chemically treated to ward off smells and control the spread of disease, ran underneath each compartment. Wooded arm supports were attached to the side walls to help one squat down.

But we couldn't complain – this was heaven in comparison to what the Royal Engineers had to put up with when they first arrived. It must have been terrible for them having to live in tents and make do while they constructed the camp in constant torrential downpours. All credit goes to them. We all took our hats off to those marvellous guys. They'd done a superb job under extremely difficult conditions and we really appreciated it. They'd worked arduously alongside the RASC, not only to construct the camp, but to make sure we had a steady water supply. All the drinking and service water was from a water tank that had been delivered by the RASC in an Austin K transporter truck.

'Brr, I don't fancy this,' I spluttered as I stripped off to wash.

'Neither do I,' moaned Pete, 'but here goes.'

The water was freezing yet refreshing as the mud flowed from our bodies down the makeshift drainage holes.

'By 'eck I feel better now,' I said, as I put on some fresh clothes. 'I only hope my bed's comfy.' That was wishful thinking.

When we returned to our hut it was dimly lit by a Tilly lamp and the atmosphere was stifling. This part of Africa was renowned for having the most humid climate in the world and it certainly lived up to its reputation. The slightest effort caused me to sweat profusely and I couldn't get any respite from the clamminess. The place was rife with mosquitoes, and to make matters worse the loud chirping of crickets seemed to pierce the eardrums. I wasn't the only one affected by the relentless high-pitched noise.

'How the bloody hell are we supposed to sleep with all that racket going on?' moaned Rodney.

'Stuff some cotton wool in your ears,' said Spud Murphy. 'That's what I do.'

'I've already done that and it hasn't made a scrap o' difference.'

'Does anybody know how to tuck these mosquito nets in?' asked Maurice, who was very fastidious and always went to bed early, 'It's rather awkward from inside the net.'

'O-ooh... rather awkward, is it?' laughed Spud Murphy, mimicking Maurice's posh accent. 'You'll have to struggle like everybody else. Anyway, make sure you check in between the sheets for tarantulas – they're as big as your fist.'

'Oh no, not spiders!' blurted Maurice, jumping back out of bed in panic. 'I hate 'em!'

I understood how he felt: a shudder ran down my spine at the very thought of a big hairy creature crawling about in my bed. I'd always had a fear of spiders, even little ones back home, and just the idea of a tarantula made me cringe.

When I was a young boy I used to go every week to the Saturday matinee and loved to watch my hero, Tarzan. He starred in weekly episodes which always finished with him in a perilous situation, leaving me in suspense until the following week. But on one occasion the chapter ended where Tarzan entered a dark cave and got ensnared in a giant spider's web, with the hideous creature moving ever nearer to suck his blood. I never slept a wink that night and had nightmares for the rest of the week. It frightened me so much that I didn't go to the pictures the following week, but I was still intrigued and asked my friends what happened. They just laughed and called me a cry baby.

While sailing over on the *Devonshire* I'd discussed my phobia with Maurice and he'd confessed that he too dreaded the furry things. So I understood exactly how he felt on this occasion, but all the same I couldn't help but laugh at his instinctive impulse to undo his mosquito net and whip back the sheets – it had us all in stitches. All the same, he made sure to make up his bed properly and he meticulously smoothed out the sheets with his hands, feeling for any bumps or lumps before climbing back into it.

'You'll have to get used to things like that,' laughed Rob. 'There are loads o' snakes, scorpions and other creatures in this neck o' the woods – or should I say jungle.'

The ribbing continued until we heard the bugler playing the Last Post. However, nobody could sleep because of the humidity and the conversation got around to our new sergeant.

'Has everybody met her now?' Pete asked.

'I haven't,' replied Mark.

'Oh, you're in for a treat,' said Rob. 'She's a real good-looker.'

'*What*? Is she a woman then?'

'No, is she hell as like! But she certainly acts like one.'

'You're having me on – he can't be all that bad.'

'Let's put it this way – if you're ever in the showers, make sure it's a cold one,' joked Spud Murphy as he downed a can of beer. 'And whatever you do, don't drop your soap or Flossie will have you, ha ha ha!'

Once again I sprang to his defence but no matter how I tried, in my mind I kept referring to him as 'her'.

'Leave it be, John – just go with the flow,' laughed Pete. 'I wonder if Sergeant Flossie will come and tuck us in before we go to sleep? Goodnight everybody… sleep tight.'

'Ah well,' I thought before finally nodding off. 'At least they're a friendly bunch – that'll make my stay out here in Africa a lot better.'

I woke up the next morning to the sound of torrential rain pounding on the tin roof and water pouring in everywhere, flooding the concrete floor.

'Bloody hell!' I thought as I put my boots on. 'How the flamin' 'eck am I supposed to keep these clean for inspection parade? By the time I've nipped across to the canteen through all that sludge they'll be as muddy as ever.'

When we were stationed at Plymouth we'd all been under the

direct command of Colonel Peck, but here at Kumba the Commanding Officer was an infantryman. All medics were still under the indirect command of Colonel Peck but he was stationed at Buea. Our immediate medical officer here at Kumba was Lieutenant Whittaker, a medical officer.

Luckily the RSM on parade was in a good mood and gave us some leeway. 'Right, you scruffy lot! I'm going to be lenient with you as far as your boots are concerned due to the muddy conditions, but that doesn't mean to say you can get away with not shaving. As from now I'm going to work your butts off for as long as it takes to get this camp up and running and shipshape.' Turning his attention to me, he barked, 'Right, medic, now give every single one of these pathetic critters a Paludrine tablet and make damn sure they swallow it! Understand?'

'Yes, sir. Understood, sir.'

The heavy rain continued and by the time I got to the hospital at the far side of the camp to meet up with the other medics I was drenched, but I counted myself lucky to be working in the confines of the hospital.

'Blooming' 'eck,' I said to Pete. 'I wouldn't like to be an infantryman, working out in that deluge. At least we're under cover.'

'No, neither would I. They'll be like drowned rats before long.'

'Right, everyone, can I have your attention, please!' shouted the sergeant.

'Here we go,' said Pete, 'Flossie's calling.'

'Flossie' was to stick for the duration of our time in the

Cameroons, but the nickname wasn't derogatory – it just became natural to refer to him that way. Even if a high-ranking officer enquired about him, the answer would be, 'Oh, she's in the sergeant's mess' or 'I don't know where she is', or something similar. They couldn't put us on a charge for insubordination because they used to answer in the same way: 'Oh, is she?' Out of respect, we never addressed him personally in that manner but always as sergeant. He was, however, aware of his nickname and far from being offended by it, he seemed to preen himself more and proudly trip about the hospital wards with a new swing in his walk. It appeared as though he had gone all lah-di-dah on us.

Evidently anxious to assert his authority, the sergeant called us to attention. 'Right, everybody! Listen carefully while I go over your duties. I'm Sergeant Burtonshaw and I bear total responsibility for the smooth running of this field hospital. Corporal Murphy will be my second-in-command and I trust I will have the support of you all while working alongside us. Between the remaining seven of you, you'll not only have to cover all nursing aspects of this hospital, which involves keeping the ward covered 24 hours a day, 7 days a week, but you'll also be on standby in readiness to go out on patrol. For every 20 infantrymen sent out to police the jungle, one medic will be attached to them. We've no patients at present but once we have, one of you will have to work night duty. I'll work out a rota so that everyone does his fair share.'

'Blimey,' said Pete, nudging me. 'We're going to have to work our balls off!'

'During your working hours,' the sergeant continued, 'some local natives, employed by the Army solely in an auxiliary capacity, will assist you. They have been briefed to carry out your orders, but remember this: they are ultimately my responsibility. I will work alongside you on the day shift, but during unsociable hours you will have to contact me at the sergeants' mess. You will also work hand-in-glove with the medical officer, Dr Whittaker, who will run a clinic every morning. I'd like to think that we're going to be one big happy family. Remember, a happy team makes a proficient team.' He paused a little before adding, 'Are there any questions?'

'Yes, Sarge,' said Rodney. 'Which one of us will have to go out on patrol first?'

'Good question, Private Marsh,' replied the sergeant, trying to remember everyone's name. 'Well, that'll fall to anyone who's not on duty at the time, and don't forget you may be called upon in the middle of the night.'

'The middle of the night, Sarge?' I asked. 'That begs the question – do we have to do guard duty?'

'I thought someone might ask that question, Private Cowell. Well, you'll be pleased to know that the answer is no… not while you're on hospital duty.'

'Great!' I said, along with the others.

'What did you mean when you said the natives have only been employed in an auxiliary capacity?' asked Rob.

'Well, Private MacNaughton, that means they're here just to assist you but they're not allowed to do any nursing duties. Any more questions?'

'Yes, Sarge,' I put in. 'What are we gonna do today without any patients?'

'Don't fret yourself about that, soldier. I'll find plenty to keep you busy.'

'Keep your gob shut, John!' whispered Bill, prodding me in the back.

'What was that, Private Hubhoard?' the sergeant asked. 'Am I missing something?'

'No. Sorry, Sarge – I was just saying to John that it'll give us a chance to familiarise ourselves with the layout of the hospital.'

'Good,' the sergeant smiled. 'I'm glad to see you're taking an interest.'

'You wormed yourself out of that one, you crafty sod,' I whispered back.

The entrance to the hospital had a narrow passageway leading off to a doctor's surgery, a treatment room and finally a ward with 10 beds. This is where the sergeant introduced us to our local assistants – Dominic, Nelson, Mathias, George, Alphonso and Kinton – and what a friendly, happy bunch they were.

This was our first chance to talk to the local inhabitants, and I welcomed the opportunity. From the word go they were so polite and easy to get on with. All six made it clear that they welcomed our presence in their country because of the many years they'd been oppressed under rule from Nigeria.

The morning passed quickly and before we knew it the bugler was calling us to dinner. Rob had to stay behind while the remainder of us trudged across to the canteen. It was during this brief respite that I met Pius Tashi, a young boy in his early teens. He greeted me after dinner as I entered our hut.

'Hello,' I replied. 'Who are you then?'

'I Pius Tashi,' he smiled. 'I like to work for you... I work very hard.'

'That's all very well,' I said. 'But what puzzles me is – how did you get past the security of the gates to the camp?'

'Oh, I come with other boys with boss man who has permit papers for us to work,' he replied politely.

'I don't know anything about that, but I tell you what, Pius,' I said to him. 'Just hang about here for a minute and I'll go and check things out – I won't be long.'

'Thank you, sir. I wait for you to come back,' he replied with a smile on his face.

'Whoa, there's no need for all that "sir" stuff, young fellow, I'm just a private soldier.'

On checking it out I found that a group of young boys had been brought along to the camp by a town official to help find work for the youngsters. The Army had given permission for them to seek work on the camp, but was not prepared to pay them personally. So I made my way back to our hut where Pius was patiently waiting.

'Right, Pius, nice to meet you,' I said, after gathering my thoughts. 'I'm John, but I'm sorry, all the hospital workers from your village are employed by the Army and they don't want to hire any more.'

'No, you no understand Mr John... I no want to work in hospital, I want to work here in hut.'

'Hang on a minute! How do you mean, you'd like to work in the hut?'

'Every day I wash clothes, I make beds, I clean boots and keep hut tidy.'

By now I'd got the idea and this got me interested. 'All right, young fellow, it sounds good to me, but now for the million-dollar question – who pays you and how much?'

'Everybody in hut pay Mr John, but only three shillings each, every Friday. I work for you six days a week.'

'That seems fair enough to me,' I replied, 'but I can't promise you anything until I've had a word with my hut mates.' At that remark a frown appeared on the lad's face. 'Don't be alarmed,' I assured him. 'They'll be back shortly and I'm sure it will be all right.'

Within a couple of minutes they had all returned and I explained the situation to them.

'I'm not paying three shillings a week outta my pay,' moaned Rodney. 'The laundry will do my washing for nothing.'

'Trust you to come up with that one, you bloody skinflint!' said Bill.

'I think it's good value for money,' I said. 'It's worth that just for cleaning our boots.'

'Yeah, so do I,' said Pete. 'Let's have a vote on it.'

Apart from Rodney, the vote was unanimous in the young boy's favour and he made his feelings very clear, especially to me.

'Thank you, Mr John, you very good man, I want you be my friend.'

'Whoa! Slow down, Pius. Let's wait and see how you get on before you think I'm your friend. If we fire you next week, you won't like me very much then, will you?'

'Fire me, Mr John?' he asked anxiously. 'I no like fire… you no burn me.'

We all burst out laughing at this. In his confusion Pius wasn't amused, but when we pointed out to him what we meant, he started laughing too.

Over the next few months our hut boy proved invaluable. He was worth his weight in gold and deserved every penny we gave him and more besides. The monsoon seemed to last forever, but no matter how muddy our boots were at the end of the day, they were sparkling clean the following morning. Because of the constant humidity everyone was prone to irritating skin rashes caused by prickly heat, especially between the groins, which meant having to change our underpants twice daily. Consequently, every day a line full of white underpants could be seen blowing on a line outside our hut. Lots of infantry soldiers became infected with the fungal-type infection, which became known as D'hobi rash, but not one medic suffered it.

'Now, aren't you glad we employed Pius Tashi?' Rob teased Rodney. 'You'd have had the screaming habdabs by now but for that boy. The laundry's a dead loss and they put too much bloody starch in the water anyway.'

Everybody on the camp, including sergeants and officers, took a leaf out of our book, employing a hut boy to do their chores. They became real assets to the camp.

For the first few days we never had a minute to spare. Even in our off-duty time we had to get stuck in with infantrymen, helping to make the hospital more accessible by chopping down trees, laying concrete paths or anything else necessary. In this we were hampered by the constant heavy downpours, which turned the mud into slush as we trudged through the camp. The heat was unbearable and the humidity drained my energy levels. After planting just a few small shrubs outside the entrance to the hospital I was completely exhausted. I wasn't alone, because all the lads were constantly laid out on their beds.

In the meantime we worked alongside the doctor as he ran the morning surgery and carried out his orders in the treatment room. Our first batch of patients were some infantrymen suffering from heat exhaustion and dehydration. Every single one of them complained that even a little effort rendered them dead beat. This ailment became commonplace as we all had to adjust to our new surroundings, something that would take at least two weeks.

The most common ailment was fungal rash, which we treated with talcum powder and Whitfield cream, advising each soldier on the importance of personal hygiene. In extreme cases the doctor prescribed antibiotics. It wasn't a serious condition but it caused a lot of ribbing among the troops. If any lad contracted it, the others would say things like, 'U-ugh, get away from me – I don't want to catch the dreaded Dengi fever!' or 'Hey, look at that fungi in between your groins – you could bloody well grow mushrooms in it!' or 'It looks like he's been bit with crabs!'

Then came the complaints of the 'bad boys' suffering the consequences of enjoying themselves with the local ladies. Many men were going frantic and couldn't stop scratching, as they suffered constant itching caused by pubic lice. As soon as the men dropped their pants, the tiny varmints could easily be seen scurrying among the pubic hairs. The main treatment for ridding them of the critters was to shave the pubic and scrotal area completely until they were like babies again. Thankfully this remedy worked within a couple of days – much to their relief.

'I'm sorry, Joe,' I said, as I examined one soldier, 'there's only one cure for this.'

'What's that?' he asked anxiously.

'Well, I'm afraid we're gonna have to cut 'em off.'

'*What*? Not my balls – *please* don't say my balls!'

I paused for a moment but couldn't keep up the pretence. 'No, Joe, you silly sod – your hairs, your *pubic* hairs!'

'O-ooph, thank goodness for that! You had me scared there for a minute!'

'Well, you will put things where you're not supposed to,' I laughed.

'Aye I know, but it's the last time, believe me.'

'Yeah,' I chuckled, 'that's what they all say. You'll be back.'

The next complaint in line – and far more serious – was gonorrhea, again caused by sleeping around with the ladies. This time the treatment was more severe.

'Drop your pants and let's have a look,' I'd say as each man in turn entered, red-faced. The most obvious sign was pus, oozing from the urethra. In the early stages the medical officer prescribed a course of penicillin injections into the backside, twice daily for a week. This usually worked but if it didn't, the doctor then prescribed streptomycin injections, which always did.

Before coming to Kumba, the only injection I'd ever given was a practice one into an orange, so I was a bit nervous at my first real-life attempt. I'd been taught in training school always to insert the needle into the upper outer quarter of the buttocks, so as to avoid damaging the sciatic nerve that runs off the spine and down either leg. In the event, all went well. I never felt a thing and the patient didn't complain. After that I never suffered from nerves again and I gave dozens of injections every week.

One day, one of the native workers approached me rather sheepishly.

'What's up, Kinton? You look worried.'

'It very bad, Mr John,' he uttered, with his head down. 'I very sad.'

'Well, what is it? I asked curiously.

'It be... I.... I... u-um.'

'Come on, Kinton! Spit it out – it can't be all that bad.'

'It is jig-a-jig, Mr John... I have jig-a-jig with lady and now I think I die.'

I nearly started laughing but I could tell by his face that he was deadly serious. 'Oh, I know what it is,' I smiled, trying to make light of it. 'You've got a poorly winkle, haven't you?'

'How you know, Mr John?'

'Never mind how I know – just drop your pants and let me have a look.'

Sure enough, just like the soldiers he had the telltale signs. I knew that I couldn't treat him officially, but I was his only hope of getting treatment.

'Right, Kinton,' I reassured him. 'It's not all that serious and I can help you, but you must keep this our little secret. I'll get thrown in jail if the doctor finds out – understood?'

'I understand Mr John, I no tell anyone... you good man.'

'You'll not think so when I give you an injection,' I laughed. 'Now drop your pants again!'

After the shot he was all smiles and sang my praises. 'That no bad... it no hurt,' he giggled.

'I wouldn't laugh yet, because you'll need plenty more before you've done.'

'That all right... I come here everyday till better.'

'There's just one more thing, Kinton,' I said, as he was about to leave.

'What that, Mr John?'

'Be a good lad,' I joked. 'No more jig-a-jig with the ladies, eh?'

'Ha ha ha!' he laughed, now a much happier man.

During the first fortnight we had to deal with cuts, bruises, insect bites, sunburn, boils and other minor ailments, but then we had a crisis on our hands – soldiers came down with symptoms of malaria. Before the end of the third week, five of the hospital beds were taken up. To top it all, two medics were sent out on patrol along with the infantry, leaving just six of us to cover the ward and other duties. Three of the patients had typical malaria symptoms accompanied by diarrhoea, nausea and vomiting.

With the aid of Dominic, I did my first bed bath on a semi-comatose patient. Remembering my training, I talked the auxiliary through the procedure, stressing the importance of treating the patient's pressure areas.

'It's very important that we turn him every two hours to prevent the skin breaking down and becoming infected. If I'm busy at the time, don't forget to remind me,' I stressed, as I turned the patient onto his left side. The strict routine was especially important in the tropical climate: the healing process took much longer in the humid conditions.

'I no forget, Mr John,' said conscientious Dominic.

He didn't, either, and it was just as well, because two hours later I was busy elsewhere attending to another patient. I was really grateful and complimented him on his efficiency. After we turned the soldier onto his right side, I did a four-hourly observation check.

'Blimey,' I thought, 'he's got a rip-roaring temperature and he's sweating like a pig!'

'Something wrong, Mr John?' asked Dominic, rather concerned.

'Yes, there is, Dominic. This soldier is poorly and needs sponging down. Can you please bring me a bowl of cold water and a sponge?'

'Yes Mr John. I go right away, Mr John! I go!'

'Whoa! Just slow down a bit, Dominic,' I reassured him. 'No need for alarm – he'll be all right.'

'Thank you, Mr John, thank you... I go fetch now.'

That's what these natives were like – obliging, courteous and friendly, and always willing to please. Their humility really impressed me.

Things turned out well and within days my patient had improved and was feeling much better. It was a valuable learning experience for me, and an opportunity to build up good relations with the auxiliaries – not that I needed to; they were superb.

My colleagues and I were only nursing orderlies but the intensive training we had undertaken held us in good stead as we carried out many and varied duties. Besides giving injections we had to treat deep wounds, becoming experts in the art of suturing. Bandaging and checking temperatures, pulses, respiration and blood pressures were all part of a day's work. It soon became apparent, however, that we had to deal with one very common complaint. Soldiers were constantly returning from patrols with deep lacerations, especially to their arms. Some of the wounds were really nasty and needed several stitches. It seemed incredible that the injuries were caused while pushing through tall grass in the jungle, but this grass stood well over six feet high and was known to the locals as 'elephant grass'.

The QUARANCs were fully qualified State Registered Nurses but we never saw them in Kumba as they were all stationed at the main campsite in Buea. My workmates and I were glad of this because the officer status bestowed on them had gone to their heads, making them unbearable to work under. It always struck me as unfair that any woman entering the Army as a qualified

State Registered Nurse was automatically promoted to the rank of second lieutenant, whereas a man with the same qualifications was only promoted to sergeant.

To me it was unfair on two counts: First, a second lieutenant enjoyed the privileges of a commissioned officer, who one had to salute, but a sergeant's status was that of a non-commissioned officer. Second, the way I saw it, an officer's pay was substantially higher than that of a sergeant. It became the topic of conversation in our tent.

'I don't think it's fair,' said Bill. 'Why those bitches get preferential treatment over men is beyond me. I like women but I haven't come across a decent QUARANC yet, the pompous bitches!'

'I know what you mean,' I said. 'They're really toffee-nosed cows, aren't they?'

'They are that! The way they pranced about on the *Devonshire* like prima donnas got right up my nose. I could gladly strangle the lot of 'em. It might be hot and clammy stuck out here in the middle of the jungle but we should all count ourselves lucky that we're not stationed at Buea. I hear them bitches are strutting about like bantam cocks, giving orders left, right and centre, and having the medics running about like blue-arsed flies.'

'I can just imagine big Bri working under them bitches,' I chuckled. 'He'll hate being ordered around. He doesn't like hard work at the best of times, so he won't like taking orders from women – especially them sort.'

'Rather them than us, eh?' Pete laughed. 'Sergeant Flossie

doesn't seem so bad now, does she? Anyway, she's got the same qualifications as them fancy pieces, so how come she's not a second lieutenant?'

'Because she – sorry, I mean *he* – is a man,' I said. 'Have you not been listening to what we've been saying?'

'I know she, he or whoever is a man,' said Pete, 'but that still doesn't answer the question, does it?'

At this point Maurice intervened. 'If you want to know the reason, it's a protective rank to stop men fronting up to women.'

'How do you know that?' I asked.

'Because I've read about it in some Army manual. Anyway, what difference does it make how I know it? I just do.'

'A protective rank?' put in Pete. 'They don't need protecting. I wouldn't touch 'em with a bloody barge pole! No way!'

'Neither would I,' added Spud Murphy. 'I've been around QUARANCS for a while now and I've never come across a good one yet.'

For the grand finale we all agreed that we were better off than our mates at Buea and that Sergeant Flossie wasn't so bad after all.

During my free time I liked going to the market about a mile from camp. There, haggling was common practice and I soon learned never to give the asking price. I could have bought two wooden elephants for what I paid for the one on the ship when we were docked at Dakar! Still, I put it down to experience. All the traders tried to sell me their wares, insisting theirs were the best. Many stalls displayed wooden carvings of animals, warriors holding spears, clocks and many other items. I was intrigued by the intricate details of each piece, which must have taken many hours and infinite patience to make – the craftsmanship was certainly first class. I'd have loved to buy many items but knew it was pointless, as I wouldn't be able to get them home.

There were many food stalls, including ones selling freshly baked bread and an assortment of tropical fruit. The meat was definitely fresh, as farmers herded cattle to market and slaughtered them to order, slitting the animal's throats in the market place and letting the blood flow into the dirt. It was not a nice scene to witness, but to the natives it was an everyday occurrence. The carcasses were then cut up and displayed on the meat stalls with millions of flies buzzing around, while the stallholder was often fast asleep. It was only a small village, yet many large wagons carrying gigantic logs used to roar through it over the potholed road at an alarming rate.

The market was on the fringe of the village, with about 40 stalls set up by the side of a fast-flowing river. This river was the border separating the British colonies from the French Cameroons. A large stone bridge spanned the water, giving access to French territory, but to us soldiers it was strictly out of bounds unless we were on special patrols. Every time I looked across towards the French side, it fascinated me. I don't know why because it looked exactly the same over there as it did on our side. Maybe it was because of the unknown or simply that it was out of bounds – who knows?

I actually crossed over the bridge every Sunday morning to

attend the Catholic service, but along with other churchgoers, I was driven there in a three-ton Bedford truck. The church was usually packed to capacity and the locals always gave us a rapturous reception; in fact, they reserved a line of seats for us on the front row. I couldn't understand the sermon totally, as the priest spoke in French. I did, however, get the gist of the Gospel and I could follow the flow of the Mass because, as a child, I'd been brought up listening to it spoken in Latin. The ringing of bells, prior to and during the offertory, were just the same as back home.

I enjoyed mixing with the locals after Mass but generally, as soon as the service was over, my mates and I were immediately driven back to camp. Lots of missionary nuns always attended the ceremony and on the forthcoming New Year's Day I decided to buy a Sunday missal and get each of the spiritual ladies and a couple of priests to sign it for me.

Kumba was only a small village, with mud huts strewn mainly alongside the one and only gritty road and others scattered here and there in the thick undergrowth. I counted three bars, two small stores and an old brick building, which housed the post office and the Bank of Kumba. The bars, set back from the road surrounded by banana trees, were the favourite haunts of the troops. I used to frequent them but always found it rather daunting as I made my way home at night along the dark dirt track, especially if it was a moonless night. It was also creepy because I had to pass the local prison, which was about half a mile from the camp and sometimes I thought I heard a prisoner screaming. But it's happen as well there was only one road to camp, because otherwise I'm sure some of us lads would have got lost after having a few drinks.

Maurice was definitely the most fastidious lad I'd ever come across. His bed space and belongings were always immaculate, earning him the reputation of Fuss Pot. I used to say my prayers before I went to sleep but to avoid ridicule from my hut mates, I would often say them quietly underneath the bedclothes. Not Maurice. It didn't matter who was there, he would unashamedly kneel down by the side of his bed and recite his offering before retiring. He didn't drink or smoke and always went to bed before nine o'clock. Next morning he would be up like a lark and ready to go before anyone else. He wasn't one for fooling around, but he was a likeable bloke and a very conscientious worker, precise in everything he did.

One night while he was taking a shower, four of us were playing cards on one of the beds and we decided to have a joke at his expense. Lizards were forever darting in and out of the hut, scavenging for food, and they were massive. Pete had recently captured one and had it in a cage under his bed. A beautiful creature, green and blue in colour with black spots, it measured about 10 inches from head to tail. It put me in mind of a small prehistoric creature as its forked tongue slithered in and out of its mouth like a snake.

'How about putting it in Maurice's bed before he comes back?' said Pete. 'It'll be a good laugh.'

'Good idea,' I agreed. 'Come on then, we'll have to be quick, though – he should be back any minute.'

'Right,' said Bill, carefully pulling part of the mosquito net out and fumbling with the bedclothes. 'Put it in between the sheets now.'

'Make sure you put everything back neat and tidy,' said Spud Murphy, wanting to get in on the act, 'or he'll smell a rat – you know how faddy he is.'

We finished in the nick of time and sat back around the bed playing cards.

'D'you want to join in, Maurice?' I asked, seeking to distract him as he entered the hut wearing a towel around his waist.

'No, thanks. I appreciate the offer but I want to go to bed; I'm bushed.'

We carried on, acting as normally as we could with one eye on the cards and one eye on Maurice's bed. First of all he got down on his knees and said his prayers and then, still in the kneeling position, carefully pulled out just enough mosquito net to allow himself to crawl under it and into his bed. Once inside the net, he drew back the top sheet and carefully edged himself underneath the bedclothes.

'Will one of you tuck my mosquito net in, please?' he asked.

'Yeah, righto – I'll do it for you,' I said, struggling to keep my face straight. 'Just give me a minute.'

'Thanks, John, you're a good lad. I'll do the same for you sometime,' he said, making me feel guilty.

After doing my little deed I quietly retreated to play cards with the lads again. Nothing happened for a while, which got us to thinking the lizard must have escaped, but then all hell let loose. At first Maurice just grunted but then he let out a piercing scream and couldn't get out of bed fast enough. He threw back the bedclothes and in his hurry pulled down the mosquito net, ripping it.

'You set of bastards!' he roared, along with a few more obscenities. We all rolled about laughing; it was hilarious to see him struggling under the collapsed mosquito net. But Maurice wasn't amused and he tore a strip off us. 'Don't think you're gonna get away with this, you scruffy, mingy gits!' he bawled. 'I'll get my own back on you if it's the last thing I do!'

He did as well, and I was his first victim.

He went about it very cleverly, catching me off guard about two months later, just before Christmas when I'd forgotten all about the incident. I was sitting on my bed and he came over to me with a carton of cigarettes in his hand – or so I thought.

'Could you give me a bit of advice, John?' he asked in his usual polite manner. 'I'm not quite sure what to do.'

'Aye, course I will, Maurice. What is it?'

'D'you think my dad would like these for a Christmas present?' he asked, handing me the carton.

'He should do if he's a smoker... I can't see why not.'

'Yes, but these aren't English cigarettes. I bought them on the market and they're brown. Will you just have a look at them for me?'

I never suspected a thing. The lid was tight and it came off with a jolt. To my horror, eight long furry legs suddenly appeared over the side, followed by an enormous black hairy body.

'A-ar-rrgh!' I screeched, frozen to the spot as a monstrous tarantula dropped onto my lap. 'Get the bloody horrible thing away from me!'

I then moved quicker than I'd ever moved in my life, cringing as I saw the horrible black monster scurrying across the floor.

'Ha ha ha!' roared Maurice. 'Got you! Serves you bloody well right!'

He'd done his homework all right. His memory of my phobia of spiders, especially big ones like that, had served him well.

He got his own back on the others too. Pete got a snake in his bed, and Bill and Spud Murphy had a bed full of ants.

We all decided it was best to leave Maurice to his quiet, unassuming ways in future.

One day, while working with Kinton, he asked me if I liked swimming.

'Yes, Kinton,' I enthused. 'Why's that?'

'I know very good place, Mr John... you like very much.'

'You don't mean the river, do you?'

'No, not river... it is a big... u-um, how you say, "lagon"?'

'A *lagoon*?' I queried. 'Do you mean like a lake?'

'Yes, very big, Mr John... lagoon.'

'And whereabouts is this lagoon then?'

'No very far... same as market, but other way.'

'Righto,' I said, becoming interested. 'When can you take me?'

'I no work Thursday… If you like I come for you.'

'Great! I'm working the afternoon shift then – what time can you get here?'

'I see you at ten o'clock, Mr. John… you have plenty good time.'

'Hey, you're not trying to fix me up with a woman, are you?'

He looked a little confused, answering, 'I no understand, Mr John… we go swimming.'

'Right,' I laughed. 'Don't take any notice of me, I'm only joking. Anyway, I'll see you at ten o'clock, and while we're at it, you can drop the "Mr John" bit.'

'Yes, all right, I no let you down… thank you very much, Mr John.'

Sure enough, at ten o'clock, Kinton was there on the dot. On leaving the camp gates we turned right, heading in the opposite direction to the market. He took a little detour from the road, and after walking for about 25 minutes through dense jungle we came to a breach, which gave way to a magnificent sight. There amid the forest was a large lake, surrounded by idyllic hills blooming with a myriad of beautiful flowers and set among green vegetation. It reminded me of a film I'd seen years previously, *The Blue Lagoon*, starring Jean Simmons; it turned out to be a crater lake of an extinct volcano.

'What about that!' I stuttered in disbelief. The cooling water looked like Shangri-la. 'I'm having some of that, Kinton – come on, let's go!'

The setting was perfect. There was even a wooden jetty set out onto the lake with a diving board, and 50 yards from the shore was a floating platform anchored by a length of mooring rope. It turned out that some European business people had built it for their own personal use but had recently left. I couldn't wait. I stripped off immediately, dived off the jetty and swam across to the floating platform.

'Come on, Kinton,' I laughed. 'This is great!'
He didn't need any encouraging and for the next two hours we had a fantastic time.

The hideaway became my favourite spot and over the coming months I whiled away many an hour there in my free time.

On one occasion I was relaxing on the floating platform, listening to the sound of the birds, when I heard some boys shouting for help. One of the youngsters had dived from the board and was in obvious difficulty, splashing desperately in the deep water. I immediately dived in and swam to him, taking hold of his arms and dragging him to the safety of the shore. After putting my First Aid expertise to full use and clearing his throat, I could see he was all right. He coughed and spluttered a little, but I knew he'd be fine. I stayed around for another hour to keep an eye on him, but within 20 minutes he was playing with the other boys again and getting up to mischief. I was happy with the outcome and felt very good inside as I made my way back to camp.

I thought that was the end of the matter but two days later I had visitors. A local couple came to the hut to see me and brought me a bottle of wine. I didn't feel a reward was necessary, but the poor

113

kind people insisted, saying they would be most hurt if I refused. Once again I was taken aback by their simple humility and even more so when they came out with something that will stay with me until the day I die.

'Mr John, you save life of our son – now he is your son too. You responsible for him all the days of his life... not his body but his spirit.'

I was touched by the gesture and their kind sincerity, and promised to keep the boy in my prayers – after all, I was now his godfather.

At the time I didn't tell anyone about the incident. It was to be my special secret and my own private legacy, and it instilled me with confidence and made me feel happy inside. Many a time thereafter, if ever I was feeling low, I drew strength from it. To this day I often think of that little boy and wonder what became of him.

Despite the hard work and unsociable hours, I genuinely enjoyed my work in the hospital and the camaraderie, especially now that the monsoon season had given way to bright sunshine. There was one aspect of Army life, however, that I didn't like at all – going out on patrol. I'll never forget the first time. I got roused out of bed at 0100 hours, and after being shepherded into the back of two Bedford trucks along with a signalman, 20 infantrymen, a corporal, a sergeant, an officer and a local native tracker, I was driven over the bridge and dropped deep into the French Cameroons. The trucks slowed down to a snail's pace allowing us all to jump for it. The sergeant immediately gave out orders, spacing us so that we wouldn't be easy targets should we come under attack. The first rays of the sun began to filter through the thick overhead green canopy and clouds of steam rose from the rotting vegetation in response to the change in temperature. I tagged along behind the courageous soldiers like a spare part as they trudged through swamps and pushed their way through thick jungle vegetation. As I pushed aside branches thickly laden with large leaves I was terrified of coming into contact with a snake or brushing up against a tarantula.

Every infantryman was encumbered with a full battle pack on his back and carried a self-loading rifle (SLR), which was deadly accurate up to 2,000 yards. But the officers and NCOs each carried a Sterling machine gun, which was more effective in close combat. It could fire 20 rounds of ammunition all at once, or one at a time in quick succession, but was only deadly up to about 50 yards. And here I was carrying the First Aid pack. In a way I was glad that I didn't carry a gun because, put to the test, I felt I couldn't shoot anyone. 'Never mind,' I thought. 'If we get attacked I'll just have to strangle 'em with my bare hands.'

All joking aside, I was scared and very wary of being shot by a sniper or being ambushed. Walking at the back of soldiers in single file through thick undergrowth was frightening, as in all the films I'd seen about jungle warfare, it was always the man at the back who got his throat slit first. Actually, none of the soldiers liked being the back man, or Tail End Charlie as they used to call it. Not having any option, I marched behind the 23 soldiers and the tracker as they hacked their way through thick bush country and then waded across a river.

As we trudged waist-height through weeds we stirred up lots of mud, creating an abhorrent smell that clung to my nostrils making me feel sick. At least it took my mind off being grabbed by a large snake or another vile creature. At the far side of the river we were confronted with yet more thicket.

'Come on, John,' I mumbled, trying to spur myself on. 'You can do it.' Despite these attempts to reassure myself I still felt very uneasy and frightened. My nerves were on edge and my imagination ran riot as I picked up every little sound, which seemed to be magnified a hundred fold. Fireflies flickered and danced to the piercing music of crickets and croaking frogs. I was used to this sound from back at Kumba, but I nearly jumped out of my skin when a load of monkeys started screeching high up in the trees. It's just as well that I didn't have a gun because I might have let off a few rounds. We'd only been marching a few hours and already I had a crick in my neck caused by constantly peering over my shoulder. To put it mildly, I was scared to death, imagining that I'd never see another day. I wondered what I was doing there: I just didn't seem to fit in at all… I felt useless. But by the end of this patrol I was to change my mind.

After traipsing till daylight, the officer called us to a halt so he could check his compass and reconnoitre the area.

One cocky lad, who also happened to be out on his first patrol, approached me and asked wryly, 'So, medic, how are you going to defend yourself if we get attacked?'

'I'll have to hit 'em with my handbag,' I joked, for want of anything better to say.

'Bloody good reply, medic,' laughed Bob Clayton, a regular soldier who was as strong as an ox and had loads of combat experience. 'I like it.' He then turned to the cynical lad and actually blasted him on my behalf. 'You've a lot to learn, you bloody sprog, so keep your bloody stupid remarks to yourself! When you've done as many patrols as I have, you'll know that the one man you need to have around in the jungle is a medic.'

The bloke didn't take too kindly to being rebuked and, judging by the way he glared at me, I got the message that Bob's advice had fallen on deaf ears.

Not to worry, there are worse troubles at sea, I thought. Then I smiled to myself. Maybe I'm not so useless after all.

My train of thought was broken by the officer issuing further orders. 'Right, men! Playtime's over – let's get going!'

We marched for ages, passing solitary mud huts way out in the middle of nowhere.

'It amazes me,' I said, 'how anyone can possibly survive in this wilderness, miles from anywhere.'

'They probably live off bananas,' laughed Bob. 'There's loads of banana trees everywhere.' It was then that we came across a small patch of land that had been ploughed. 'There you are, medic,' he said. 'It looks like they've got their own tiny allotment.'

'What are those tall things growing in the crop?' I asked naively. 'They look like pineapples.'

'They *are* pineapples, you silly sod,' laughed the corporal. 'Are you thick or what?'

'But I thought that pineapples grew on trees, like apples – I didn't know they grew in the ground.'

'Well, you know now, you daft bugger!'

Up until that point I'd always assumed they grew on palm trees, as their trunks look like large pineapples. 'Ah well,' I thought, 'something else to store in my memory box.'

Every now and again we'd come across large columns of ants on the march. They would appear from the undergrowth and disappear into the thick jungle foliage some hundred yards further along the track. The columns were about five inches wide and made up mainly of workers, but soldier ants patrolled their flanks keeping them in position. There must have been millions of them, but they didn't bother us if we kept out of their way.

During a short break some soldiers started to lark about and put some lit cigarette ends right in the middle of a cluster, just to see what would happen. Immediately the workers scattered in confusion but within seconds a number of soldier ants threw themselves onto the burning remnants and smothered the flame. Other soldier ants immediately removed the carcasses and the stubs while others reorganised the column. Within minutes they were back on the march as though nothing had happened.

'You silly bastards!' roared the sergeant. 'What have I told you about messing about with them critters? We'll have to move on now or else they could be swarming all over us – and believe you me, if you get bit by one of them soldier ants you'll know about it! It's a lot worse than a bee sting.'

I don't know whether they would have attacked us or not, but at the time it did seem the best thing to trek on.

As we pushed on, my throat became parched but I only dared to take a sip to wet my lips as my water bottle was already well down. I could gladly have drunk it all there and then, but the veterans had stressed time and time again the importance of conserving water. That small sip tasted like nectar and I was tempted to take a big gulp but knew better of it. It did, however, test my willpower to the hilt. Eventually at noon we had to stop, as the sun was now directly above us and it felt as though we were in an oven. Despite sitting in the shade of the thick foliage and the green canopy above, I couldn't get any respite from the unrelenting heat.

'Bloomin' 'eck,' I groaned as sweat oozed from every pore. 'I'm bloody well baking!'

'You're not the only one, medic,' rapped the same bloke who'd had a dig at me earlier. 'Anyway, what are you moaning about, you flea bag? You're supposed to be the one looking after us!'

I was too knackered to get into a dispute and just replied flippantly, 'Yeah, all right – keep your hat on. Oops, sorry – I mean your hair!'

'Too bloody true I'll keep my hat on! I don't need you to tell me that,' he sneered, not catching on to what I meant. At that a few lads started laughing and defused the situation.

I could understand the lad being ratty because I felt that way myself. I was clapped out, dehydrated, clammy and the humidity was unbearable. To make matters worse, as I tried to wipe the sweat from my brow I noticed some bloody fat leeches, feeding merrily away on my arms. It was my first encounter with these vile critters and they repulsed me. What bothered me most was the fact that I'd never felt a thing when they'd attached themselves to me. It was alarming because no matter how well buttoned up we were, the leeches somehow got through to the skin.

'U-ugh!' I thought. 'How many more of these filthy creatures are attacking me?'

It soon became apparent that other soldiers had unwelcome guests as well. 'Quick, medic, give me something to get rid of these varmints!' they screeched.

'Just burn 'em with the lit end of a cigarette, you bunch of sissies,' laughed Bob. 'They'll soon drop off.'

'That's all right, but how the hell do we keep 'em off?' yelled one lad.

'I don't know about leeches,' I said, 'but I've got loads of insect repellent in my bag. Maybe that'll work.'

'Gimme some!' yelled several at once. 'Owt's worth a try.'

'I don't know what you're nattered about,' laughed Bob. 'Just watch this.'

As it happened he had one attached to his right forearm and it didn't bother him in the slightest. After a short while we could see it swelling up like a balloon as it filled with blood. It then turned a bright red in colour and when it seemed near to bursting, it simply dropped off.

'U-ug-gh,' groaned one of the lads. 'It's a bloody bloodsucker, just like a vampire! I couldn't stand that.'

'What are you on about? Don't be so bloody soft,' Bob laughed all the more. 'It's only like having a blood transfusion. They reckon it's good for you to give a pint of blood and that's enough to feed a thousand bloody leeches.'

'You may be right,' said one of the lads, applying some insect repellent to his arms, 'but I'd rather keep 'em at bay. They give me the creeps.'

During our respite the officer posted some men on guard and advised the rest of us to get our heads down to catch up on some sleep.

'He must be joking,' I thought, 'with all these creepy crawlies about.' That's what I thought, but within five minutes I was in the land of nod along with the others. I was just about to dive into an icy-cool swimming pool when my dream came to an abrupt end.

'Come on, you scruffy lot! Bedtime's over,' ordered the sergeant. 'We've a lot of marching to do.'

Deep into the jungle, we moved at a slow pace as the front lads hacked their way through the thick undergrowth with machetes. At one point we came to a full stop as thick masses of foliage made it almost impossible to proceed. The officer called a halt to assess his calculations using an Army compass. A couple of veterans and the native tracker acted as scouts and each in turn slashed vigorously away at the strong foliage to pave the way. Communication between the scouts and the officer was constant as they worked as a team; their expertise and innate ability to survive was second to none.

After trekking for hours through the sweltering jungle, we came across an almost dried-up river bed with a scattering of stagnant pools. Much to our despair they were infested with midgies and mosquitoes. We badly needed to rest but had to crash on regardless because these flies were more irritating than the leeches. We ploughed our way through some elephant grass but the plague seemed to follow us. Once again Bob Clayton's experience came to the fore.

'I know the mosquitoes are irritating, lads,' he warned, 'but don't try rushing through this elephant grass or you'll finish up cut to pieces.'

He was right too because this batch of grass had been well baked by the hot sun, making it really brittle and each blade was like a razor's edge.

'Bloomin' 'eck,' I thought. 'I know now why they call them blades of grass. These blades are bloody lethal!'

It was only when we began to climb a steep incline that the swarm died down and left us in peace. Only when we were well clear of these tiny pests did the officer order a halt. The leeches and other creepy crawlies were bad enough to cope with, but then we encountered another disgusting critter.

'Ar-rg-gh,' screeched one of the soldiers as we sat taking a breather. 'What the bloody hell's this on my arm!' It was a tick. This was the first time I'd come across one and it made me cringe. I'd been told about them in training school but my knowledge was limited. I did know, though, that if I didn't remove it the soldier could be in trouble. The vile creature, about the size of a cherry stone, had buried itself beneath the skin. It had already burrowed its way an inch up his arm and left a snail-like trail of slimy eggs.

'I'm sorry, mate,' I said. 'I can't just burn it off with a cigarette like we do with leeches; I'm going to have to cut it out.'

'I don't care!' he panicked. 'Just get rid of the horrible thing!'

I rummaged through my medical bag and pulled out a packet of Gillette razor blades. 'One of these will do,' I thought. At least they'll be clean. I then tried to put the lad at ease. 'Right, mate. First, I'm going to have to make a tiny slit at one side of the tick and then try to scoop it out with a penknife. I'm sorry, but I can't numb it for you 'cos I haven't got any anaesthetic on me.'

'Oh, flamin' Emma! Is it going to hurt?'

'Well, yeah, but I'll be as gentle as I can.'

'All right then – just get on with it!'

I'd never dealt with a tick before but I was aware that they had crablike legs and that it was vital I didn't leave any remnants inside; otherwise he could get blood poisoning. After dousing the area with iodine I nervously made a slash at one side of the parasite and then attempted to dig it out with the knife.

'Ouch!' he winced. 'Be quick!'

I prodded about as carefully as I could until I felt as though I was underneath its body and then gently eased it out.

'Is that it, medic? Have you got it?'

'Not quite – there's still a couple of legs stuck in there and some eggs. Just bear with me for a while longer,' I assured him as I picked out one of the scrawny limbs with a pair of tweezers. Surprisingly, both legs came out smoothly, just leaving me to flush out the eggs and other crap. 'That's it!' I said, feeling pleased with myself. 'It's all done and dusted. All you need now is a plaster to keep the wound clean.'

'Thank goodness for that,' he sighed. 'I can't stand the little parasites.'

Not long afterwards the officer called us to task and once again we were on our way. For a while we climbed steadily, finally arriving at a ridge just as the sun was setting. We were all weary and dishevelled, but thankfully the officer called a halt while he carried out another reconnaissance of the area. After thoroughly reviewing the situation, he issued further orders.

'Right, men,' he murmured softly. 'This is the place I've been looking for. About 500 yards along this track the ridge overlooks a hamlet of about 20 huts and according to intelligence they're harbouring some guerillas. I want you all to bivouac down here now for the night because we're going to swoop down on them just before dawn tomorrow. Now you've all been drilled constantly for this type of operation, so you know the score – no talking, communicate by whispering or sign language if you have to. The sun rises at 0600 hours so I want you all alert by 0500. That's all for now – I'll give further orders then.'

Before dismissing us, he deployed four men to stand guard and keep watch for any sign of guerilla activity.

'Blimey,' I thought. 'It's all right saying we've been drilled for this – *I* bloomin' well haven't!' I placed my Army cloak around my shoulders and bedded down on a sloping mound of grassland, but I couldn't settle as once again anxiety started to build up inside me. It seemed so unreal that I was actually going into action alongside these courageous infantrymen. 'Bloomin' 'eck,' I trembled inwardly. 'Some of us might be killed tomorrow and one of them could be me…' My fear intensified when it occurred to me that if we knew the guerillas' whereabouts, then they might have information regarding our coming and could be waiting in readiness to ambush us.

My thoughts wandered back to my childhood when my grandad used to tell me tales of the time he spent in the trenches on the Western Front during the First World War. At that moment I realised how he must have felt on the nights before he went on the offensive against the Germans. Then suddenly I was brought back to reality.

'Ouch!' I gasped as thousands of ants started to crawl all over me, biting like hell. Along with my comrades, I had to strip off and douse myself with loads of insect repellent, which thankfully kept them at bay. I didn't get a wink of sleep that night but it wasn't nerves or insects that kept me awake – it was the cold. It was absolutely freezing. 'I don't believe this,' I muttered through chattering teeth. 'I was baking this afternoon and now I'm freezing to death!'

Sure enough, before the crack of dawn the officer ordered us to converge onto the small village and muster all the people together. My anxiety was soon laid to rest, as the soldiers worked furtively together using sign language. I would learn more about jungle code in the next few hours than in all my Army experience.

The soldiers did their job well. After stealthily negotiating the steep grassy hillside on their backsides, gradually they encroached upon the tiny hamlet and took it over without any resistance. After searching every hut thoroughly, the troops rounded up the unsuspecting natives and herded them together. I hated this part, as adrenaline sent some of the soldiers power-crazy, and they prodded the males savagely with the butts of their rifles and aggressively ordered them to lay spread-eagled and face down on the ground.

Meanwhile, frightened and bewildered small children clung to their mothers' clothing, wondering what was happening and sobbing their hearts out. I felt awful and ashamed as I saw the look of sheer horror on the faces of the terrified women, some of whom were bare-breasted and holding crying babies in their arms. I'll never forget their petrified expressions as they stood there, quaking with fear. Other soldiers bawled loudly and held loaded rifles at the ready, pointing them at the poor inhabitants who obviously thought they were going to die.

I couldn't help but think I didn't know these soldiers. They were totally different to the friendly bunch of lads I had grown to know. Their hateful expressions with screwed-up eyes and snarling mouths gave them a totally different demeanour. To me they were no longer acting like decent human beings but more like savages, a frenzied mob... and I was part of it. It seemed deplorable to treat our fellow men in this way.

'What am I doing here?' I thought. 'None of these poor souls look like tyrants to me – they're just ordinary families trying to survive the best way they can.' During the short spell I'd spent in Africa the Cameroonians had become my friends and here I was helping to round them up like animals in the most appalling and degrading way. A strong feeling of disgust overtook me and I felt sick in the pit of my stomach, but I tried to convince myself it was a necessary evil.

It so happened that the soldiers detained four men who turned out to be known rebels, but even that didn't ease the feeling of guilt in my heart. Despite the fact that we found some antiquated weapons, I still felt bad about it. But as far as the Army was concerned, the entire operation was a success, without one round of ammunition being fired off.

By the time we'd made our way back to the top of the ridge with the insurgents, who were made to carry the confiscated weapons, the sun had risen, revealing a sight to behold. There, stretched out in front of me as far as the eye could see, were miles and miles of jungle, which I hadn't been able to detect in the dark. It wasn't the most beautiful sight I'd ever seen, but it was certainly the most unusual as the thick mass of trees swayed in the wind, making ripples like waves on the ocean. Just as the horizon on the Atlantic had looked like the end of the world, so too did this – the only difference being that this ocean was green instead of blue.

On the way back my expertise again came in handy as two lads badly needed stitches to deep lacerations in their forearms – again the cause was elephant grass. One of the lads happened to be the sprog, and after being patched up, he became a little friendlier towards me.

127

After handing the guerillas over to the Nigerian police, we made our way back to camp. The first thing I did when I got there was to get rid of my stinking clothes and have a shower.

On returning to my hut, Pius Tashi gave me a warm greeting. 'All right, Mr John? It is nice for you to be back.'

'And it's good to be back, Pius, and nice to see you!'

'Now you rest, Mr John, while I wash your clothes and clean boots.'

'Thank you very much, Pius — you're great,' I said, lying on my bunk. Before I drifted off, I looked up at the corrugated tin roof and felt like I was in heaven.

That was my first taste of a patrol and I have to admit I didn't relish the thought of doing any more. Even so, just like my comrades, I had to do my fair share during the following months. However, unlike my first experience I didn't have to sleep out in the open.

B Company, which covered the vast jungle area around Kumba, was made up of three platoons — 4, 5 and 6. Usually two platoons would be out on patrol duty in regions like Tombel and Edibinjok, which were coffee and cocoa plantations, while the other one guarded the camp. Sometimes we kipped down for the night in barns on the plantations but mostly, if we were away from camp for a few days at a time, we billeted in a large fortress-type building in Essosong. While out with 5 Platoon, Sergeant Bull, a veteran of the Second World War, told me that it was known as a German *schloss*.

This stone castle, which had been built by the Germans before the First World War, now served as a very useful outstation for our lads. It was ideally set up with sleeping quarters and running water, and it stood in idyllic surroundings. After a hard day's trekking around the jungle it was an ideal retreat and very comforting to return home to. There was even an upstairs section that was bunked out. Because of the home comforts, some of the lads nicknamed it Shangri-la.

There was another reason why the lads and I enjoyed it so much. One of the locals, in his early forties, had the job of warden and kept an eye on the place at all times. He happened to have a couple of daughters and it soon became apparent to the lads that he wasn't quite so vigilant with them. His house stood about 50 yards from the fortress in the middle of a smallholding, where he kept chickens, goats and other livestock. It was easily overlooked from the battlements and, much to the amusement of the troops, the two young girls used to sunbathe regularly in scanty bikinis in the garden area. Lots of lads would stand on the ramparts from where they had a bird's eye view of the two bathing beauties and wave their shirts in the air. Some soldiers would cheer excitedly and make innuendos in an effort to prompt the girls to bare all. The girls appeared to enjoy the attention and would make certain gestures, which only spurred the lads on even more.

The parents of the two youngsters must have known what was going on because we could plainly see from the ramparts into their dining area where they ate around a large table. To my knowledge nothing more went on, but this simple display used to send the lads wild. At night time it was certainly a talking point over a can of lager and, without a doubt, was good for morale.

During the coming months the outpost proved to be very efficient, and while I was with B Company, the troops policed the surrounding areas successfully, arresting many guerillas, illegal immigrants and smugglers. On one mission, my Burnley mate Martin Grogan went on patrol with 5 Platoon who, along with some Nigerian policemen, took over a guerilla camp and arrested at least 20 suspected rebels. The camp was ingenious and self-sufficient in every aspect, housing livestock and growing food products. Due to careful planning and skillful tactics, the infantry lads easily took the camp with little resistance and within a short time had rounded up all the renegades. Once in custody, the guerillas made no attempt to escape, as they knew full well that the Nigerian police wouldn't think twice about shooting them dead on the spot.

On routine patrols the infantry did their own policing with the help of a native tracker. Sometimes we came across some locals doing a bit of poaching, simply to survive. The officer in charge usually let these pitiful blokes off with a caution, knowing full well that if he handed them over to the Nigerian police the unfortunate men would be in big trouble. This really proved to me that the squad was only seeking the real offenders and it eased my conscience somewhat.

Every guy in the platoon agreed that poaching in order to survive and feed his family was acceptable, but there was one incident that repulsed every single one of us. Throughout my time in Africa I never ever saw an elephant roaming in its natural habitat, but sadly I came across a dead one. It was the most dreadful, horrific sight. The poor creature was a young bull almost fully grown and it had been shot and its tusks had been ripped out.

Unlike the poor natives who poached to survive, these poachers were savages in every sense of the word. They'd committed this despicable crime and killed a magnificent animal purely for greed and gain. Also they'd chosen their victim carefully because the ivory tusks would have been almost fully grown and in perfect condition. The felons by now must have been well out of harm's way because the pathetic carcass was half-eaten by buzzards and other jungle animals. It was the most ghastly sight I'd ever seen and I felt sick to the pit of my stomach. I wasn't alone, as all the other lads were outraged as well. It was just as well that the ruffians were not about because if the soldiers had caught them at that moment I'm sure they would have shot them or hung them from the nearest tree. Our signalman got on his radio right away and reported the incident back to a camp official, who in turn passed it on to the local police.

'Good,' growled one of the infantrymen. 'I wouldn't like to be in their shoes now. The Nigerian police and jungle trackers will hunt them down relentlessly until they catch 'em.'

'They'll string 'em up and roast 'em over an open fire,' said another.

'I hope so,' roared others. 'Serves 'em bloody well right! They deserve all they get, the bloody bastards.'

When we got back to camp that night the topic was discussed among the men and they all agreed that the act was vile and hoped that the aggressors would get their comeuppance.

On one occasion we came across a camp of a few deserted huts, which contained many knives, spears, makeshift swords, blow pipes with poison arrows and some primitive guns. After destroying the camp the weapons were confiscated and shared out among the men as souvenirs.

One patrol I went on was uneventful in terms of catching any guerillas, but it's one I will never forget. We saw neither hide nor hair of the enemy but the officer in charge decided that they were hiding in swampland. After instructing everyone to use the jungle code, he waded into the swamp and ordered us to follow. I hated it and was frightened to death as I followed into the everglade up to my knees, struggling to keep my medical bag high and dry. Aware that the mangroves were the ideal habitat for crocodiles, I had visions of being dragged down into the muddy depth by one of these vicious creatures.

As I dragged myself through the swamp the sun climbed to its height, making rivulets of sweat run down my face. The temperature must have risen to 130 degrees, making the task unbearable. Salty sweat and the glare of the sun reflecting off the water made my eyes smart. I didn't know whether it was a wise thing to do, but I soaked my hat in the smelly swamp and doused my face with it in an attempt to ease the stinging. It seemed to help a little bit and must have been alright because most of the other lads did the same. The intolerable heat caused vapour to rise from the swamp giving it a ghostly appearance, which caused further trepidation. The deeper we trudged into the swamp, the more the undergrowth seemed to grow in profusion. It was apparent from the other men's mannerisms that I wasn't the only one feeling agitated. The nauseating stench of rotting vegetation was obviously getting to everyone... it was absolutely repulsive. Progress was extremely slow as we splashed our way stealthily through slime and rotting vegetation, striving to negotiate the thick, fibrous roots of mangroves. Every time I mis-negotiated the roots I plunged up to my waist in slimy mud. I kept dragging myself up only to plunge back in within a few steps. Even when I found a footing the roots were slippy and treacherous. Adding to these problems, the mosquitoes were out in full force and clearly were having a whale of a time feasting on us. After toiling for about two hours the officer finally decided to give up the hunt and turn back. I think he realised that even if the guerillas were hiding somewhere in the swamp, there was no way of capturing them. They had advantage on their side and, knowing the geography and the secrets of the jungle, they could easily have ambushed us. Besides, the signalman had slipped and his radio equipment was covered in mud and in danger of not working.

I was highly delighted with the decision as it had passed through my mind that we might have to camp out in the swamp overnight. By all accounts other platoons had had to spend several nights under such conditions. How they'd survived amazed me – we'd only been in the swamp four hours and already we all looked like clay men. I had mud in every orifice of my body and the leeches were having a field day. When we got back to camp I headed straight for a shower only to discover that my face, arms and neck were covered in pockmarks due to mosquito bites. That was my first taste of a swamp patrol and thankfully my last, but I still had to go out on routine patrols.

As we worked close to the border crossing we often came across French colonial troops patrolling the French side. They always appeared to be a mean bunch, equipped with bandoliers and camouflaged gear. We could only communicate with them using sign language from our side of a river and we never, ever crossed the border unless under special orders. We didn't feel totally at ease when we were in their vicinity, as there was something untoward about them.

Our senior NCOs, veterans of the Second World War, warned us that they were nasty pieces of work and ordered us to keep a strict vigil and be doubly alert. There were lots of inhabitants being murdered on the French side and we suspected that the French troops were the culprits, who then laid the blame on others. If any guerillas fell into their trap there was no mercy shown, and most were shot dead there and then. Even if their prisoners were only suspected guerillas it didn't seem to make any difference; their chance of survival was very slim. Life seemed to be so cheap. On returning to Kumba I exchanged experiences with my colleagues regarding different incidents, and they had similar tales to tell. We all came to the same conclusion – that the French troops were ruthless.

After a full day's patrolling the jungle in the sweltering heat it was always good to get back to the German fortress; it was a sight for sore eyes. The lads loved nothing more than to get a few beers down their throats and talk about the day's happenings and then finish up with a sing-song. They were truly courageous devoted men, professional in every way, but at the end of the day this was their way of letting off steam and relaxing. Along with a few other lads, Martin and I loved to sunbathe within the grounds of the old fortress during our off-duty time.

Overall, my workmates seemed to prefer going out on patrols to nursing duties. It always surprised me that many of the lads would actually get excited at the prospect of going out on patrol. Personally I felt much more at home and at ease within the confines of the hospital.

CHAPTER FIVE

THE WORLD CUP

I enjoyed both working alongside the happy, contented Cameroonians and mingling with them at the market and other places. They lived in impoverished conditions but would gladly have given the shirts off their backs in a crisis. One thing that stood out because of their hand-to-mouth existence was that all of them, including the children, had large pot bellies with grotesque belly buttons due to malnutrition. Because of the shortage of food the bairns were forever foraging around the camp site begging. I, along with my colleagues, used to pass them food through the wire fence surrounding the camp; this was strictly against Army policy but the lads did it anyway. How could we refuse the poor little blighters as they stood there like ragamuffins with their appealing little faces? Despite their plight these little ones had an ever-beaming smile, with pearly white teeth.

It took me back to my childhood when I, along with my mates, used to stand outside Burnley Fire Station and scrounge meat pies and cakes. But this was far more serious because, although I was brought up in poverty, we were always assured of at least one good meal a day. It might have only been a school dinner but it was nourishing and sustaining, whereas these poor souls could go for days, or maybe weeks without having a proper meal.

We soldiers were well fed in the camp, and lots of food was wasted and used as pig swill in the same way as it was in schools back home. It got me to thinking just how much these youngsters would appreciate what we were throwing away. I didn't actually collect anything from the pig swill, but I did gather remnants left over on plates such as pies, potatoes and bread. Besides feeding the food through the wire fence, we sometimes used to give it to Pius Tashi, our hut boy, who appreciated it immensely.

Despite their fate of being born into squalor and having to follow in the same footsteps as their parents in their impoverished existence, the young ones always appeared happy. I know they didn't know anything different and seemed to accept their lot as normal, but I couldn't help but compare them with children the same age back home. It made my blood boil to think of all the money that was being spent on armaments and defence, not just by my own country, but by the Cameroon government as well. It came across as clear as crystal that the powers that be just didn't give a damn about these poor people.

The women did most of the home chores and could readily be seen carrying large water containers balanced precariously on their heads, never spilling a drop. The scene reminded me of the song that Harry Belafonte used to sing:

Oh, island in the sun
Willed to me by my father's hand,
All my days I will live in praise
Of your forest's waters and shining sand.
I see woman on bended knee
Cutting cane for her family,
I see man by the water side
Catching fish by the rising tide.

As the women went about their daily tasks it seemed as though the song had been written especially about them.

The men were more into sport, especially football, which had been instilled into them from an early age. Young boys happily played on dirt tracks using a small rubber ball the size of a tennis ball – and good they were, too. Many a time I enjoyed watching them play competitively, adeptly using skills I'd never seen before.

As it happened, Pete and I enjoyed playing the game, and as there were some decent players among the infantry mob, we formed teams and played against each other. Martin Grogan was an exceptional player, much better than me, and so was always guaranteed a game. I'd played alongside him back home in Burnley during my teenage years for Sandygate Youth Club. Being a natural player and a prolific goalscorer, he'd always been an automatic choice in the youth team, whereas I'd spent many hours as a reserve. Out here in Africa, history seemed to be repeating itself, as I participated in many matches solely on the sidelines.

Word of the football games spread through the camp and some of the native workers asked if they could join in. After a few sessions the reputation of our football team spread further afield and ultimately the village council approached the camp, inviting us to play their local team.

We all accepted eagerly and looked forward to the challenge, but I was in for a disappointment. On this day of all days, I happened to be on duty. I certainly wouldn't have got into the team but I would have loved to watch the game. Martin and Pete were both obvious choices and went to the match with a smile on their faces. I was unhappy about missing the occasion, but when the lads got back after the game Martin gave me a detailed account.

Our team had been rather complacent about the whole affair, taking it for granted that the match would be a walkover. What an awakening they got. The Cameroon team was made up from specially selected players from various towns and villages within the region, and nearly 4,000 spectators turned up from far and wide to watch their squad play a team of super-fit men.

On the day of the match our lads turned up with two nets, two football strips, an assortment of football boots and some buckets and sponges. Considering they were playing the equivalent of a county team in England, the lads were expecting to play on a top-notch pitch. But it was not to be – the playing field was more like a building site in a forest clearing, with potholes everywhere. The goal posts and the bar were cut from thickets, and the dressing room was a cluster of banana trees. But the biggest shock of all was Cameroon's football strip. Our side ran onto the pitch wearing blue-and-white kits, but the natives lined up in shorts and nothing else. Not one of their players had a pair of football boots between them, yet they stood there ready to take us on in their bare feet.

'I can't believe this,' said Martin. 'How can they possibly expect to play against us with nowt on their feet? We'll murder 'em.'

All our lads started laughing and wanted to call the game off but the locals wouldn't have it. 'No, no, we play... we give you plenty good game.' They were adamant, pointing out that they always played in their bare feet.

'But some of you are bound to get injured,' protested Pete.

'Yeah,' agreed Martin. 'Our lads will be doing sliding tackles and their studded boots could easily crush a foot – especially a bare one.'

'That's right – it doesn't bear thinking about,' our captain added. 'Some of your lads could be maimed.'

Still, the natives remained insistent. 'No, no,' said their spokesperson, 'we be all right, we play plenty times against teams with boots.'

The rest of the Cameroon team started chanting cheekily, 'You afraid we win' before adding, 'We take care not to hurt you.'

Their persistence and determination to play prevailed, so the game got underway. But first of all our lads got together and mustered a red strip and 5 pairs of football boots.

'There's an odd boot here,' said Martin as he rummaged through the back of our truck.

'An odd boot's no good,' quipped Pete. 'They can't do anything with that!'

He couldn't have been more wrong. As we handed over the trivial gift, the Kumba team expressed their delight by hugging all the soldiers.

'Now with boots we beat you easily,' they grinned impudently as they ran back to the banana trees.

'I don't know why they're so happy,' said Pete. 'They still need another six pairs. I wonder which players will wear the boots?'

'Probably the forwards,' replied Martin.

'I think the defenders will wear them, to help them tackle better,' responded Pete.

They were both wrong, but what a laugh everybody got. As the Kumba lads took to the pitch, three of them were wearing a pair of boots, but five of them wore just one boot each.

'Bloomin' 'eck!' laughed Martin. 'That's the funniest thing I've ever seen in my life! I can't believe it!'

'Neither can I!' roared Pete. 'It's hilarious. Come on, let's get out there and wop 'em.'

But any preconceptions our lads had harboured about the game before it started were soon quashed and by the end they were under no illusions. The courageous natives threw themselves into the match, pouncing like tigers for every ball. Boots or no boots, they weren't afraid of going in for a tackle.

Despite their determination, Martin took a good cross from the right wing and scored a brilliant header with only five minutes gone. Not to be outdone, the Cameroonians fought back and within minutes they had equalised. Joyous shouts resounded through the air, accompanied by the loud beating of drums and squawking parrots. The game continued, but despite every team member playing with complete determination, the score remained 1-1 after 45 minutes.

At the break, our visibly shaken squad knew they had a tough second half on their hands. 'Right, lads,' said our captain. 'No more complacency. Let's get out there and give it to 'em!'

The Cameroonians took the restart and the clash of the titans continued. The sides were deadlocked, but with 15 minutes to go Martin scored his second, putting us into the lead again. This time it was a rather scrappy affair. He was in the penalty area with his back to goal and surrounded by a cluster of players, but somehow he niftily back-heeled the ball through the goalkeeper's legs. For the next 14 minutes the Kumba lads pressed, hungry for an equaliser, but found themselves up against a sturdy defence. Our lads thought Martin's goal was the match-winner but the Cameroonians had other ideas and scored again with a minute to go. The whistle blew for full time with a fair 2-2 scoreline. What a game!

Some of our lads were disappointed with the outcome but they soon perked up when an official photographer arrived to take a picture for the county newspaper. Martin stood at the end of the second row while two Kumba lads sat on the front row in their bare feet. The photograph turned out brilliantly, capturing all the players and many spectators. Martin treasured that picture and rightly so, but he never dreamed that many years later, in 1990, Cameroon would be playing England in the quarter-finals of the World Cup, and that very snapshot would be printed in a national newspaper, showing both teams side-by-side, boots an' all – or no boots an' all.

The World Cup quarter final match was played on a Sunday evening, but just a week earlier there had been an article in the *News of the World* newspaper stating that England would be playing against the Cameroons for the first time. Martin wasn't having any of that, so he contacted the newspaper as living proof, telling them of the original game and the photograph. They were very interested in the story and sent a reporter to his house. After going over all the details and scrutinising the photo, the editor was highly delighted and decided to print a piece in their next edition. Sure enough, on the morning of the game they displayed the photo across the full breadth of the page and the headline read 'England 22-Cameroons 11'. The article went on to say how a British Army team had played the Africans way back in 1960 and how the natives had only had eleven boots between them.

The World Cup match was to be played that evening and the odds were stacked in England's favour. England sported a formidable team, with players like David Platt, Paul Gascoigne and Gary Lineker in the side. In the previous round against Belgium, Platt had scored a brilliant last-minute winner in extra time by volleying the ball into the top corner, leaving the goalkeeper with no chance. It was a superb strike but a lot of it was owed to the creative inspiration of Gascoigne, who had taken a free kick from the left wing, floating the ball perfectly for Platt to connect. The England side was on top form and quoted as outright favourites to go through to the semi-finals. Despite everything, Martin pointed out to the reporter that it wouldn't be an easy game by any means – and his prediction was spot on.

That night supporters of both sides sat glued to their television sets, and after 90 minutes the score was 2-2, exactly the same as the game back in Kumba. England went in front as Platt made it 1-0 and it looked as though they were going to cruise home. But then Cameroon moved up a gear, and scored two cracking goals to take the lead. The score remained at 2-1 for a period and with only eight minutes to go, England looked in serious trouble. Then fate took a hand as Lineker was brought down in the penalty area. A penalty was awarded and Lineker calmly converted the spot kick to level the game. The score remained at 2-2 until the final whistle, taking the game into extra time.

During the next 30 minutes the game remained tight but England finally won 3-2. Again Lineker was brought down in the penalty area and, much to his credit, the England forward again slotted the ball neatly into the back of the net. The win put England through to the semi finals, the best progress they'd made since winning the World Cup in 1966. But every England supporter was fully aware they had just beaten a brilliant team. The game certainly put Cameroon on the map: from being a relatively unknown country, it was now renowned and applauded worldwide.

Meanwhile, back in 1960, we went on to play every Saturday afternoon, creating a bond and a friendly atmosphere between the Cameroonians and the troops. Martin and Pete played against Kumba and other outlying villages many times; I only participated in one game but thoroughly enjoyed it. Our opponents were on form and within 20 minutes we were 2-0 down. But two minutes later Martin scored a cracker, calmly slotting the ball into the bottom corner of the net after taking on the keeper, and five minutes later he levelled the score with a bullet header from a corner kick.

At 2-2 the game remained evenly balanced, but just before half-time Kumba's centre forward scored a brilliant goal, putting the Cameroons once again in front. After receiving a perfect cross from the right wing, he controlled it on his chest, then dribbled skillfully past two defenders and slotted the ball into the bottom left-hand corner, leaving our goalkeeper helpless. My teammates and I just stood there in disbelief as about 200 local supporters jumped up and down, screaming with delight. We pressed on, but at half-time were still trailing by one goal.

In the second half we piled on the pressure but just couldn't score. Time was running out and we'd almost given up, but in the 80th minute we had a stroke of luck. Pete ran down the right wing and crossed a perfect ball towards me, but just as I was about to connect the goalkeeper fisted it away from my head. Luckily the ball bobbled on a rough piece of ground and bounced perfectly for Martin, who skilfully lobbed it over the head of the oncoming goalkeeper for his hat-trick. This stirred up the Kumba lads, making them more determined than ever to get the winner. They were a breed of their own and I couldn't help but admire their combination of unrelenting desire to win and sense of fair play. Nevertheless, they didn't score again and neither did we – again, the game finished as a draw.

I didn't work alongside Martin but we socialised, along with other friends, in the NAAFI and often went swimming in the blue lagoon. Like me, Martin enjoyed sport, the odd drink and got stuck into his work – and he too had a stubborn streak which landed him in trouble now and again. But on one occasion he got three days' jankers for the pettiest offence I ever came across.

Although he loved playing football, Martin was never keen on basketball. As it happened, Sergeant Bull, so nicknamed because of his bulky physique, was promoting the game. Two nets had been assembled in the middle of the camp and the burly sergeant was determined to form a squad of fine players. He was aware of Martin's ability on the football field and wanted him as a player in his basketball team. Martin wouldn't have minded so much but it meant that he missed out on playing football, which infuriated him – never more so than one Saturday afternoon when Sergeant Bull had a match arranged against another squad that he was determined to win. Martin was an automatic choice.

'But Sergeant,' he protested, 'I hate basketball, and anyway what about the football team? They've got a game on this afternoon.'

'Forget the blasted football team, Grogan,' bellowed the sergeant, towering over him. 'You'll play basketball and like it!'

Unlike Martin, I enjoyed the game and chatted with him as we changed into our strips.

'I'm bloody well cheesed off, John,' groaned Martin. 'I'm gonna miss out on football all because o' this crappy game!'

I really felt for him because I knew how devoted he was to his beloved football. But I was glad to be in Bull's team, as I would have only been a spare part sat on the reserve bench for the football team. All the same I found it amusing and couldn't help laughing. 'Sorry about that, Martin,' I said. 'It just struck me as funny. You know why he's done it, don't you?'

'Oh aye, 'course I do – we're playing Corporal Gallagher's team and it's a right grudge match. Bull wants to clobber 'em.'

'You've got it. Bull hates losing to him more than anybody else. You should have seen him t'other week when Gallagher's team trounced us – he was bloody furious!'

'Yeah, I heard about it. But if he thinks I'm gonna get stuck in just to inflate his ego, he can get bloody lost!'

As we lined up for the start of the game, Sergeant Bull was standing on the sidelines, but Corporal Gallagher was actually playing in the match as a defender. Only five minutes into the game I collected a ball on the right flank, bounced it past a couple of players and passed it to Martin, who was stood underneath the opposing net with Gallagher facing him. He neatly caught the ball and positioned himself to lob it upwards while Gallagher jumped up and down on the spot, waving outstretched arms to prevent him from scoring.

Martin grimaced with determination as he drew the ball back to his chest and then to everyone's amazement, he very gently threw it at Gallagher's body and dropped his wrist loosely in a camp manner, mouthing 'O-o-oooh!' with pursed lips.

Everybody on the pitch burst out laughing, but one person on the sidelines didn't see the funny side.

'Gro-o-ogan!' screeched a frenzied Bull, waving his wooden baton. 'Get your bloody arse over here now – at the double!'

Martin traipsed off the pitch to be marched to the guardroom, where he was charged with the ridiculous offence of being idle at basketball, for which he received the jankers.

Poor Martin. He begrudged every minute of his sentence but at least something good came of it – he never had to play another game of basketball. I, on the other hand, became a regular choice and took pleasure in it.

Another game I really enjoyed playing was table tennis and I was chosen to be a team player, along with two other lads. As it happened, some European businessmen threw down the gauntlet, challenging us to play their three best men. We accepted and it turned out to be a really good match. During the contest we set up the table in the NAAFI and each one of us played the opposing three players. We were evenly matched and the outcome was settled in the last game, which I lost 21-17, making the score 5-4 for the entrepreneurs.

'That was one hell of a bout,' said the opposing captain. 'We must have a return match at our clubhouse.' We did too and it was great. Unlike our sweatshop they had superb facilities and the table was set up in a large hall with all the mod cons – a fitness room, showers, air conditioning, the lot! On their home ground we reversed the score 5-4 in our favour. Once again the score was 4-4 but this time I won the last game, gaining revenge on my opponent. To finish off the night in style, we drank some ice-cold beer by the side of the swimming pool, which they said we were welcome to use during our off-duty periods.

I enjoyed the game, but the discipline at which I excelled was physical training. Pete, some infantry lads and I set up a wooden vaulting horse and other apparatus in the open air. PT was always my favourite subject at senior school: handstands, back flips, cartwheels – I revelled in them all. I was very agile and had a natural ability for it; I could easily run, spring over the vaulting horse, go into a dive and then do a back flip from the end of the box, landing on my feet. Lots of lads became interested as I did my party tricks and asked if I would train them.

Before long it became a regular exercise and even some of the native workers asked if they could participate. My fame spread beyond the camp gates and some Kumba locals, who didn't work on the camp, joined the class. It suited me perfectly and helped me to relax. As well as keeping fit and trim, I also made a lot of friends. One day I was approached by an official from Kumba town council, who asked if I would consider taking a job in Kumba once I'd finished my stint in Her Majesty's Forces. I still had six months to serve so I didn't take the proposition too seriously, but since then I've often regretted not taking them up on the offer. Who knows what might have come of it?

One night I'll never forget occurred when I went out for a quiet drink with Pete. It all started innocently enough as we sat in one of the bars chatting to the locals.

'Hello Mr John, hello Mr Pete,' came a voice from behind us. 'I no see you in this bar before.'

On turning it was Dominic, one of the camp workers.

'Hiya Dominic!' I greeted him. 'I didn't know you came in here. You live on the other side of the river in the French Cameroons, don't you?'

'That right, Mr John, but sometimes I come here to see my cousin Alberto... he own this bar.'

'Good,' laughed Pete. 'Then maybe we can have a drink on the house.'

'Drink on house?' queried Dominic, still not familiar with our expressions. 'I no understand. Why drink on house... we drink in bar?'

'Yeah,' laughed Pete with tongue in cheek. 'I like it – very funny.'

Dominic wasn't too sure what Pete was laughing at but joined in all the same. 'Yes, it is very funny, Mr Pete... very funny.'

Pete knew Dominic hadn't got the joke, making him laugh all the more.

'Where do you usually go for a drink then, Dominic?' I asked.

'Always Mr John, I take drink in bar near my home across the river… it is much bigger than this one.'

Pete's ears pricked up at this. 'How have you got here then, Dominic?'

'I come here in Jeep of my father.'

'Oh aye? Is there any chance o' taking us to this bar then?'

'Whoa, hang on a minute, Pete!' I cut in. 'The bar he's talking about is on the French side – it's out of bounds.'

'So what? Come on, John – get cool for once in your life,' grinned Pete. 'Dominic will take us and fetch us back, won't you?'

'Yes, if you like I take you and bring you back… but I no want trouble for you.'

'Oh, never mind about that,' Pete laughed. 'I'm willing to take the risk if you are, John.' 'Ay-ye, I suppose so,' I replied, once again giving in to temptation.

Impatient and raring to go, Pete downed his drink in one and made his way to the door. 'Come on, John!' he shouted eagerly. 'Let's get going! We may not get another chance.'

'Righto, I'm coming, I'm coming!'

'Good, about time! For a minute I thought you were going to back out.'

'Yeah, I would do if I'd any sense.'

'Well, you haven't. Anyway we're only young once – let's go for it!'

I went for it all right but what I saw when I got outside should have put me off. 'What the bloomin' 'eck's that?' I asked Dominic as he started to climb into a old truck that was decorated like a gypsy caravan. 'I thought you said you'd driven here in a Jeep.'

It turned out to be an old Mammi wagon that had been converted into a bus.

'It is bus of my father... You like?'

'It's a bit dilapidated, in't it? Are you sure it'll get us there?'

'What you mean, Mr John?... I no understand.'

'Take no notice of him, Dominic,' Pete butted in. 'If it gets us over the river that'll do me.'

'Hey, what about the border patrol policing the bridge?' I asked edgily.

'We'll just have to lie on the floor,' quipped Pete, quite unconcerned.

'I don't know so much – we'll never get away with it. And don't forget we've to get back across the bridge as well.'

'Oh, come on, John! Lighten up a bit, don't be such a killjoy... We'll have a great time.'

'Aye, all right,' I relented, climbing into the back of the rickety vehicle, 'but I've got a feeling I'm gonna regret this.'

As we drove towards the bridge I felt agitated at the thought of being discovered by the Regimental Police, yet excited at the prospect of doing something I shouldn't.

'Halt! Who goes there!' rapped one of the guards, ordering Dominic to stop. Pete and I lay deadly quiet hidden underneath one of the sagging seats, not daring to move a muscle.

'Hello, 'tis only me,' replied Dominic in his chirpy fashion. 'I cross river now back to my house.'

'Oh, it's you, Dominic,' said the MP. 'Have you had a good night?'

'Yes, Mr Policeman, plenty good... I take plenty beer with soldiers.'

'I'll bet you did, and what about the ladies? You have plenty jig-a-jig as well?'

Dominic played along with the conversation, laughing and joking. Thankfully, the picket never looked inside the vehicle.

'Bye bye,' said Dominic keeping his calm. 'I see you again.'

'Bloody hell, that was nerve-racking,' spluttered Pete once we were on French territory.

'You're not bloody kidding,' I replied. 'I only hope it's gonna be worth the trouble once we get there.'

Almost immediately Dominic left the road and drove for about 20 minutes over a beaten track. Shortly we arrived at a little hamlet in the thick of the jungle.

'There,' said Dominic, pointing to a large shanty-type building. 'That is bar that I tell you... it is big, no?'

'Oh, what a good do,' laughed Pete. 'Let's get in there – I can't wait!'

The French bar was far bigger than the one back in Kumba and had background music playing. I felt rather strange at first as a few locals weighed us up, but settled down when two workers from our camp acknowledged us. Time passed quickly as Pete and I thoroughly enjoyed ourselves, laughing and joking with the friendly natives. But things were about to change. I'd just finished my second drink when one of the camp workers approached us.

'You like jig-a-jig? I find you very nice ladies, you have plenty good time!'

'No, it's all right,' I answered politely, 'but thanks all the same.'

'Hey, you speak for yourself!' quipped Pete. 'I wouldn't mind a jig-a-jig. I'm feeling rampant – I haven't had a woman since we left England.'

'Come off it, Pete!' I protested. 'We could be in enough trouble as it is already. Let it be!'

My protest fell on deaf ears. Pete ignored me and questioned the man further, making it plain that he was raring to go.

'Right, Mr Pete, you come with me, I take you to hut of very sexy lady… you have plenty jig-a-jig.' Pete followed the man eagerly, and to my dismay, Dominic got up as well.

'Where are you going, Dominic?' I asked anxiously.

'I go with Mr Pete to make sure he all right.'

'Just hang on a minute! I'm not stopping here on my own! I haven't a clue where I am.'

I followed the three of them very cautiously, aware of danger and frightened of the unknown.

Sensing my apprehension, Dominic assured me there was no need for concern. 'Everything will be all right, Mr John… I just no want Mr Pete to lose way.'

I hope so. Please God, I hope so! I prayed inwardly.

After walking through thick undergrowth we stopped outside a mud hut with a straw roof among a cluster of others like it. 'You come with me,' said the man addressing Pete.

'Bloody hell, what am I doing here?' I fretted as Pete

disappeared into the scant hut. Then, to make matters worse, when I turned round Dominic wasn't there… I couldn't believe what was happening. 'Oh no,' I thought. 'It can't be… please don't say that Dominic's deserted me!' By now my nerves were on edge and I was trembling as nightmarish thoughts ran through my mind. It was the unknown factor and not knowing what to do that frightened me. But thank goodness my fears were unfounded, as a moment later I heard Dominic's voice.

'All right, Mr John, I'm with you now.'

'You're with me now! Where the flamin' 'eck have you been? You terrified the living daylights out of me!'

'I sorry, Mr John… now you come with me.'

'Hang on a minute, Dominic – where are you taking me?'

'It be all right… I take you to see nice people.'

'Aye, all right,' I replied through chattering teeth. 'I trust you.' I felt that I had no option as he took me to one of the other shanties.

As we entered the hut I found myself in a single candlelit room divided by flimsy cotton curtains. A man and his wife sat around a small round table alongside a young girl. She was about 17 and the prettiest thing I'd seen since arriving in Africa. When I looked at her she gave me a sweet, alluring smile and bowed her head. The couple offered me a drink, and despite feeling uneasy and out of place, I sat down among them.

'Hello, Mr John,' said the man. 'Me and wife very happy to meet you.'

'And I'm pleased to meet you too,' I mumbled.

'This our daughter,' said the wife. 'Her name is Sabia... she very pretty.'

'Yes, she is,' I replied politely, wondering what was going on.

As the conversation progressed I kept glancing at Sabia and she kept glancing back. I liked the look of her but under the circumstances I didn't know what to do. Then providence took a hand. The young girl slid her hand across the table, placing hers in mine. It felt nice and soft, but I couldn't help but feel uncomfortable, as her parents' eyes bore down on me.

'It is all right, Mr John,' said the lady. 'Dominic tell us you good man and our daughter... she like you.'

'Oh. Thank you very much,' I spluttered, still unsure what to do next.

'You come with me, Mr John,' said Sabia, standing up. 'We go sit alone.' She then drew back one of the flimsy curtains, revealing a bed, and enticed me towards her. I couldn't believe what was happening and still felt very awkward.

This time the man pointed to the bed, nodding. 'It is all right, Mr John, you go in private place with daughter... she like you very much.'

I went behind the curtain more out of respect and bewilderment than anything else and just sat petrified on the edge of the bed, twiddling my thumbs like a dummy. I could feel my shoes tapping the floor as my legs shook uncontrollably.

The young girl closed the curtain and sat down at my side, again taking my hand. I liked the feel of her tender touch but the uneasiness continued and I was simply frozen to the spot.

'You no like me, Mr John?' she asked, looking at me with sad, puppy-like eyes.

Her words put me in mind of the scene from the film *South Pacific*. John Kerr, a young naval officer, falls in love at first sight with a beautiful Polynesian girl. During a loving embrace she looks at him with the most appealing deep brown eyes, whereupon he takes her into his arms and starts to sing the delightful love song 'Younger Than Springtime'. But I'm afraid that in my case, romance was not to be.

My thoughts were soon interrupted as the young girl once again asked, 'You no like me, Mr John?... I good girl, I make you good wife.' Her eyes, despite being sad, were sparkling and vibrant.

'Yes, of course I like you, Sabia, but –'

But I didn't get to finish my sentence as a great commotion erupted outside the hut and I could hear men shouting in an aggressive manner. Suddenly three natives came bursting into the room, one of them wielding a machete. Luckily for me, the two workers came onto the scene and intervened, striving to calm the situation down. But the man holding the weapon couldn't be reasoned with and he screamed out in a frenzy: 'I kill white man who take my woman... I kill... I kill!'

The next thing I knew, Pete was in the hut, challenging the man to a fight.

'Don't be crazy, Pete!' I shouted across the room. 'Use your loaf, for crying out loud! We're in the middle of nowhere – if you start something here we'll be slaughtered!'

Thankfully the truth of what I was saying dawned on him and, realising the gravity of the situation, he took heed. 'Bloody hell, John, you're not wrong. Let's get the hell out of here!'

So we scarpered away from the huts as fast as we could, heading hopefully back towards the border. It was a dark night but luckily we hit the dirt road and ran with the screaming natives in hot pursuit. It was horrible – I was actually living my worst nightmare, as I knew that at least one of the natives had a machete. After running blindly for about half a mile we heard a friendly vehicle horn – thank goodness it was Dominic.

'Good lad,' I panted as he pulled up besides us. 'Get us outa here as quick as you can!'

'I sorry, Mr John, Mr Pete, for causing you to have trouble.'

'Don't worry about that now,' grunted Pete. 'Just get going, for crying out loud!'

'Phew, that was a close call,' I sighed as we left our pursuers behind.

'Aye, you're right there,' puffed Pete. 'We'd have been dead meat if they'd have caught us – they would have cut us to ribbons.'

'Yeah, especially the one with the machete – he wasn't in the mood for messing about.'

'We're not out of the woods yet, John. We've still got to get past the border patrol – if they spot us, we're up the creek.'

'Tell me something I don't know! It's your bloody fault that we were there in the first place. Anyroad, I couldn't care less any more. Even if they do spot us, that's nowt compared to what could have happened back there.'

'We'll cross that bridge when we come to it,' smirked Pete, trying to play down the situation.

'Ha ha, very funny. Is that supposed to be a joke? Anyroad, we'll soon find out – I can see it now in the distance.'

As we approached the river Pete and I had to crouch down again under the seats. Thankfully luck was on our side. The guards had changed over and the new ones, who didn't suspect a thing, let Dominic pass through the barrier without any fuss. Pete and I sighed with relief as the bus drove off, knowing we'd got off lightly.

'Blimey, Pete,' I said. 'We got away with murder there, didn't we?'

'Oh, I don't know so much,' he quipped. 'You could actually say we got away with *not* being murdered!'

'Very good, I like it – you're on form tonight, Pete.'

We laughed as we passed the Kumba bar where our little escapade had begun, but we were both highly delighted to see the camp gates.

'Oh what a beautiful sight,' I said. 'I never thought I'd be so happy to see them again.'

'How's it going, lads?' one of our mates shouted from the guardroom as we passed through the barrier. 'Another boring night in the backwoods?'

'Yeah,' I shouted back. 'Just another humdrum night!'

'Little do they know,' Pete laughed as we made our way to our hut.

'Aye, you're right there – and tell 'em nowt. After all that rumpus I can't wait to hit the sack in peace and quiet.'

I never again ventured out of bounds, as it didn't hold the same fascination any more. But every time I crossed over the bridge on official business it brought back memories of that night… and, of course, Sabia.

It was Christmas before we knew it and we decorated the hut with tinsel and Christmas cards from back home. The Army very generously supplied us with small regimental Christmas cards with a map of the British Cameroons printed on the inside cover. The map showed Victoria, where the *Devonshire* had anchored up, and clearly displayed the camps, Buea, Kumba, Bamenda and the Air Force base at Mamfe. I liked the card so much that I sent one home to my mum.

Some soldiers formed an entertainment committee and staged a few shows and a pantomime in the NAAFI, while the Army put on films in the open air. The feeling of watching a film under the stars was fantastic. It created a good atmosphere and boosted everyone's morale. I especially enjoyed the first film which, under the circumstances, was very appropriate: *The League of Gentlemen*, starring Jack Hawkins. It was about a high-ranking officer who was very disgruntled about the way the Army had retired him. He conjured up a plan to rob a bank by using the expertise of other retired soldiers, all highly skilled in their different departments. His plan was flawless, and the way he conned the Army and relieved them of some arms and ammunition had every one of us in raptures. Despite perfect planning, the plot failed, but I enjoyed it all the same.

Christmas dinner was different because the commissioned officers waited on tables; a longstanding tradition. There were no party hats or Christmas crackers but we still had a laugh because most of the troops were off duty. Some lads were unlucky enough to be on fatigue duty, but even they only had to do a couple of hours. After eating to the point of nearly bursting I felt guilty, thinking of the poor little blighters outside the camp who might not have anything to eat at all. So without giving it a second thought I obtained a cardboard box and filled it to the brim with loads of bread, potatoes and some turkey leftovers. Sure enough, there they were, waiting for their little treats. It made my day to see the big smiling beams on their faces; you'd have thought they'd just won a thousand pounds. I got so carried away that I forgot to watch my back, and I got caught by one of the MPs.

'Soldier! What d'you think you're playing at?' he roared.

'Oh no – I'm up for the high jump if he charges me,' I thought. 'Surely he could let it go for once… it's Christmas Day.'

He must have read my thoughts or maybe he'd had a good present from back home; maybe he might have even felt sorry for the little blighters, I don't know. What I do know is he seemed to relent and after reading me the riot act, he let me off with a caution.

That night it was like payday in the NAAFI as we all celebrated to the sound of musical love songs and downed a few cans. The camaraderie among the men was fantastic, taking into account that most of them had never set eyes on each other only a year before. Every soldier missed home and always looked forward to mail from England, especially so at this festive time of year. Some of the lads received treats from home but they gladly shared them among all the men. Everybody laughed merrily as they exchanged happenings from back home and showed photographs of their wives, children and sweethearts. It was very stirring to see these tough young men reading their letters with tears rolling down their cheeks. There's no doubt that letters meant so much to everyone in the camp and they were a real boost to the men's morale. That is, of course, if it was a love note and not a dreaded 'Dear John' letter. Not many lads received a DJL, but when one did, he would be completely devastated and there'd be no consoling him. Luckily, no one received one over the Christmas period.

We celebrated Christmas well, but New Year's Eve left an everlasting mark on my memory. My nursing colleagues and I decided to put on a party for the troops, using the clinical room and part of the hospital ward. We worked in league with the Catering Corps and each one of us had a simple task to perform. The infantry soon got wind of the party and some offered to help. My job, along with Jock Hulston from Stirling in Scotland, was making up various sandwiches. He was a driver in the Service Corps and it soon became apparent that he was a character. He'd brought a bottle of scotch and from the start he took a brisk drink and offered me a tot of the amber liquid.

'Cheers, mun!' he said, raising his glass before downing his dram in one.

Wanting to be sociable I did the same, whereupon he immediately refilled my glass.

'Whoa!' I said, knowing full well this was going to be a long night.

'Dunno be so daft, get it down your throoat – it'll do yee the world o' good.'

'But I...'

'No boots, mun! Tonite is New Year's Eve – the best nite o' the year.'

He was very persuasive and anyway I enjoyed the burning sensation at the back of my throat.

'Right, Jock – you're on... cheers!'

'See mun, what did I tell you? I knew you'd enjoy yourself.'

'You're not kidding, mun,' I chortled, trying to imitate his Scottish accent.

'You don't mind having a drink before you have something to eat, I take it?'

'No, Jock, I don't,' I replied. 'I never like to eat on an empty stomach.'

'Ha ha ha!' he burst out laughing. 'That's a good one. Where did you dig that up from?'

'I don't know, Jock – it just came out automatically.'

'Well, it's a good one – I'll have to keep it in my joke bag... cheers!'

By the time we'd finished the sandwiches I felt tipsy and the night was still young.

Every soldier had contributed something and there was a

mountainous pile of beer cans stacked on a table. One of the lads obtained a record player along with some records from the officers' mess and soon the room was vibrating to the sound of music. By ten o'clock the hospital took on a new light, echoing to the sound of boisterous laughter from the soldiers. Two hours later Maurice collapsed onto the floor from the effects of alcohol. Four of us each took a limb, carried him back to our hut and then tucked him in underneath his mosquito net. On this occasion we decided it was wiser not to put another lizard in bed alongside him.

'Trust Maurice to be the first to flake out,' laughed Pete.

'I can't understand it,' I said. 'I've had a lot more to drink than him and I'm all right.'

'Aye maybe, John, but think on. This is the first time Maurice's ever had a drink… at least to my knowledge.'

As the night went on I became merrier and merrier, enjoying the festivities as the alcohol rid me of my inhibitions. Consequently I got carried away and did something that could have landed me in serious trouble. Captain Smith, along with some English businessmen, decided to join the party and to our surprise the civilians brought their absolutely gorgeous wives. I couldn't take my eyes off one of them as she danced around the floor in high heels and silk stockings, displaying the most beautiful pair of legs. Apart from the QUARANCS I hadn't seen a white woman since leaving the *Devonshire*. But this ravishing lady was desirable, and her very presence triggered off my hormones, especially when she danced by, sending off a whiff of perfume.

The music changed to a smoochy number and my heart pounded faster and faster. As the couple passed by, I got a strong impulse and just couldn't stop myself. Without thinking, I tapped the bloke on the shoulder.

'Excuse me, please,' I said, taking hold of the lady's arm. At first, she appeared a little surprised, but responded in a pleasant manner, making me feel at ease. As I stared into her deep blue eyes she gave me a pert smile, endearing me to her all the more. I was completely smitten.

'And what's your name, soldier boy?' she asked.

'John,' I smiled back.

'Oh, what a gorgeous smile you have and such beautiful teeth,' she murmured softly, boosting my ego.

'And you're a beautiful lady,' I answered, drawing her close to me.

She responded by caressing my shoulders with her hands and before I knew it, I was tenderly kissing her neck. Whether her husband was neglecting her I don't know, but what I do know is she enjoyed the attention and responded by kissing my cheek. As I danced by some soldiers, they expressed their delight.

'Yeah, go on John! Give her a kiss for me!'

I didn't need any encouragement. This was one 'eck of a lady and I readily grasped the moment. I was totally besotted and didn't notice the resentful look on the civilians' faces, and to tell the truth I didn't give a damn.

My moment of bliss came to an end as Captain Smith tapped me on the shoulder.

'Excuse me, soldier,' he snarled, glaring at me. 'Report to my office at 1400 hours tomorrow!'

'Please yourself,' I thought. 'I haven't broken any rules.' Turning to the lady, I smiled, 'Thank you ma'am, that was delightful... Happy New Year!'

'And the same to you, John,' she smiled back. 'Take care.'

'By 'eck that was nice,' I murmured as I walked off the floor to be greeted by some infantry lads.

'I'll bet you enjoyed that, you lucky swine,' they laughed, giving me the nod.

'I did that, lads. I think I'm in love... she's absolutely stunning.'

Just then Bill rang a bell, temporarily bringing the festivities to a halt. 'Attention everybody – it's countdown time. Get ready... Five – four – three – two – one... Happy New Year!'

Everyone began to sing 'Auld Lang Syne' and during the celebrations I made my way towards the gorgeous lady to offer her my best wishes and a New Year's kiss. But there was no chance – the officer barred my path and warned me off. 'On your way, Private Cowell. Don't push it – you're in enough trouble as it is!'

'Bullshit – up yours!' I thought. I didn't get a kiss, as the businessmen grouped together to cordon her off, but they couldn't stop me from silently mouthing, 'Happy New Year!'

She nodded back in acknowledgement and blew me a kiss across the palm of her upturned hand, annoying the civilians even more.

My elation was interrupted as another soldier flopped to the floor in a drunken state. I couldn't believe it – this time it was Pete and he was out cold.

'Bloomin' 'eck, Bill! Who'd have thought it?' I blurted. 'Pete can really take his ale – it's not like him to flake out.'

'I know that,' laughed Bill, 'but he's been on the ale since four o'clock! He's fairly knocked back some cans.'

'Aye, so have I, but I feel all right,' I smirked.

Just as we did with Maurice, four of us each grabbed a limb and carted him back to the hut. As I tucked in the mosquito net I was convinced Pete was having us on. When we got back to the clinical room the celebrations were still in full swing but sadly, the lady of my dreams had gone, along with the captain and company.

Spud Murphy, in his own brand of humour, started to poke fun at me. 'Get some ale into your belly, John,' he advised, ''cos it's gonna be your last chance for a long while.'

'What are you talking about? I haven't done anything wrong.'

'You don't think so, do you not? All I can say is I wouldn't like to be in your shoes.'

'How come?'

'How come?' he smirked, gulping down another beer. 'Come off it! You know what a bastard that captain is – if he has his way they'll lock you up and throw away the key.'

'How can they do that? I haven't broken any Army rules.'

'Army rules, my arse! I've been in the Army for 20 years and I can tell you now it doesn't pay to get on the wrong side of a captain, especially one who's pushing for promotion.'

'Blimey,' I said, getting worried. 'Did I go that far?'

'Did you go that far? You should o' seen the look on his face when you were kissing that woman! As far as he's concerned, you've undermined his authority and showed him up in front of his friends. He was bloody frothing at the mouth!'

'Oh bloomin' 'eck!' I moaned. 'I didn't mean to do owt wrong – I was just having a good time and got carried away.'

'Bloody hell!' roared Murphy, breaking out into a fit of laughter. 'Just look at your gloomy face! I'm only joking. Mind you, I still think he'll pull you over the coals and maybe give you a few days' jankers, but that's about it. Anyway, Happy New Year! Get some more ale down you.'

'Get this in your belly, John,' said one of the lads, handing me a can of beer, 'and stuff 'em all.'

'Cheers,' I responded. 'Happy New Year!'

I don't remember a thing after that. My next recollection was waking up the following morning underneath my mosquito net with the most horrendous hangover in the world. Just like the others before me, I'd actually been carted back to my bed in a collapsed state. I couldn't lift my head off the pillow and the slightest movement made me feel like spewing my guts up. Gradually, I managed to dangle my legs over the side of the bed – to find Spud Murphy grinning at me, a can of beer in each hand.

'Here, John – have a swig o' this,' he laughed. 'The hair of the dog an' all that.'

'Ur-r-ggh!' I retched. 'Take it away – it smells awful!'

'E-eh, just look at you,' he scoffed unsympathetically, 'and you were mocking the others last night 'cos they flaked out.'

I'd no answer to that and just bent over, clasping my head in my hands and feeling sorry for myself. I tried lying down to sleep it off, but no chance. The room started to spin as all the contents of my stomach churned over, making a gurgling sound.

'O-o-hh... somebody please stop this roundabout and let me get off!'

It's a good job I wasn't on duty that day – I felt like I was dying. I'd had a hangover before but nothing like this. Maurice and Pete were still sleeping but the rest of the lads were in high spirits, laughing and joking. I could hear loud music and every beat pounded 'boom boom boom', making my temples throb. I just had to get out of the hut into the fresh air, but as soon as I took a deep breath, my stomach muscles tightened and went into spasm, causing me to retch. No matter what I did, I couldn't get any respite from that abysmal feeling and for the first time in my life I couldn't eat.

To make matters worse the captain sent word, summoning me to his office. At this point I hadn't been officially charged, but I made my way to see him full of foreboding.

'Blast it!' I mumbled to myself. 'I thought he might have let it go, what with it being New Year's Day an' all.'

Even though I didn't feel in any fit state to argue my case, I was determined to say my piece and canny enough to address him in the manner befitting an officer.

'Right, Private Cowell. What have you got to say for yourself about what happened last night?' he rapped as I stood to attention.

'I beg your pardon, sir, but I'm not quite sure what you mean,' I replied, acting innocently.

'You what!' he roared. 'Don't get clever with me, soldier, or I'll have you thrown in the brig! The way you acted with my friend's wife was appalling.'

'I'm sorry, sir, but I don't think the lady or I did anything wrong.'

'Damn you, man! *She* didn't do anything wrong but it's not her I'm on about – it's *you!*'

He'd taken the bait. This was the very thing I wanted him to say and the very manner I wanted him to say it in. He hadn't followed the Army code and so, in my mind, his aggressive manner now gave me the right to talk to him on level terms – man to man.

'Quoting your own words, she didn't do anything wrong, which means that I didn't do anything wrong either.'

'For crying out loud, Private Cowell,' he said, regaining a little composure. 'She was a guest of mine and you showed me up in company.'

'With all due respect, sir, my friends and I worked very hard organising that party for the troops. You took it on yourself to invite civilians, which indirectly makes you responsible. All I can say in my defence is that it was New Year's Eve and I was thoroughly enjoying myself. I'd drunk loads of beer with the lads and I can't deny that I was very attracted to the lady. But I must add that we didn't do anything behind closed doors – it was all in the open.'

At that I detected a slight snigger at the corner of his mouth but he suppressed it. Deep down, I suspected that he was more embarrassed than angry.

He pondered what I'd said for a while before saying, 'Go on, get out of my sight and don't let it happen again – especially in front of me!'

As I made my way back to the hut I took in a big breath of fresh air and chuckled, 'Ah well, John lad – all's well that ends well. Happy New Year!'

Relieved at the outcome but still suffering badly with the terrible hangover, I felt like taking myself off to bed but it was Sunday and I was determined to start the New Year off by attending the afternoon church service over the river. Jock Hulston, my Scottish boozing partner from the night before, offered to run me there in one of the Landrovers and we arrived in ample time. The church was packed to the doors with standing room only and the congregation sang so beautifully, with a rhythm that only African people have. On this occasion, Jock was in no hurry to get back to camp and it gave me ample opportunity to speak with the missionaries. This is when I bought the Sunday Roman Missal, which all the dear ladies signed for me. The local priest also stamped it with the official hallmark of Kumba.

I enjoyed Army routine because it took a lot of stress out of my life. I'd no major decisions to make and I had everything laid on a plate; all I had to do was follow orders. I didn't even mind the strict discipline and the pettiness, but one thing I didn't like was injustice and in my case the Army did something unforgivable.

172

Their sin against me was bad, but the way they treated one of the local natives was abysmal.

There was a corporal in the infantry and to say he was a bastard is an understatement. He was a bully, a barbaric fiend and a beast all wrapped up in one. Like all bullies he was a coward, using intimidating tactics against unsuspecting victims much smaller and weaker than himself. He was a regular soldier in his late twenties and he got away with flagrant offences for which a National Serviceman would have been locked up for. A tall man with a fine physique, weighing around 18 stones, he was forever getting drunk and throwing his weight around, using bullyboy tactics. Without a doubt he was a despicable ruffian and his reputation preceded him wherever he went. Among the troops, his nickname was Corporal Bullyboy.

One morning I happened to be on duty in the clinical room when the medical officer approached me.

'John,' he said, 'I've got a soldier here who's fallen into a ditch and badly damaged his right hand on some rocks. He's got severe lacerations to three fingers that need suturing. I'm going to start him on penicillin injections so I've told him to attend every day for a jab and a change of dressings.'

'Fine, sir, leave it with me,' I replied.

Nobody was more surprised than me when Corporal Bullyboy entered the room. When I saw his hand I actually felt sorry for him, but then he started to shoot his mouth off.

At first I made a joke of it. 'Bloomin' 'eck! You must have had a skinful last night! Did you fall into the ditch on the way home?'

He just scoffed and laughed arrogantly. 'You don't really think I did this on a rock, do you?'

'How d'you mean?' I queried. 'That's how Dr Whittaker thinks you did it.'

He sniggered again and then started to brag. 'Of course that's what the doctor thinks, you idiot! That's what I wanted him to think – for the record an' all that. I busted my hand on the thick skull of a wog, knocking his teeth out – ye-eah, I really gave it to him!'

'Why? How come?' I asked. 'What happened?'

'E-eh, me and my mates went out on the town last night and got tanked up. We were still knocking 'em back at three o'clock this morning.'

'Oh yeah? Did you get into a fight then?'

'No, did we bloody hell, but there was a nigger in there flashing his wallet about with loads o' money in it. He was getting right up my nose so I decided I was gonna have him and his money as well. My mates left but I waited outside and hid in some bushes, and when he came out I jumped him and gave him a right teddying.'

His vulgar expressions and mannerisms repulsed me, and the pity I felt for him earlier completely left me. Devoid of human compassion, he revelled in the fact that he had afflicted agony and misery on a fellow human being. He certainly didn't reflect the typical soldier, as most of the troops got on very well with the local natives, working alongside them both on and off the camp. Despite my revulsion I still had to treat him, but I wanted him to feel some pain, so I didn't administer any local anaesthetic before stitching his fingers.

'Ouch! That hurts, you bastard!' he gasped as I put three sutures into each finger. 'Can't you numb 'em first?' Although he liked to inflict pain on others, evidently he didn't enjoy it when he was on the receiving end.

I came up with an excuse. 'There's no point because the process of numbing is more painful than the actual stitching. I would have used Lignocaine if you'd needed five or more stitches in each finger.'

'Aye, all right, but get it over and done with will you, for crying out loud!'

I'd lied about the anaesthetic but I didn't care. It was worth it to hear him squeal like a pig. 'Serves you bloody right!' I thought. I then gave him an injection with the biggest needle I could find.

'Ou-uch! That hurt, you bloody little wimp! What did you use – a flaming darning needle?'

Once again I thought how he got pleasure from inflicting pain on others but, like all cowards, he didn't like pain himself.

'That's better,' he gloated, when I'd finished dressing his fingers. 'This'll give me and my mates something to laugh about.'

'You bloody bastard!' I thought, as he strutted from the treatment room as though he'd done something heroic.

I mentioned what he'd said to the medical officer but his reply was, 'You might as well let it go, John. It's just his word against yours.'

'But sir, surely it's wrong if he gets away with it scot-free?'

'I know that, but my hands are tied. I can only base my medical report on what he claims happened, and he told me he fell over on some rocks.'

I felt rather dejected as I left the surgery, but that wasn't the end of it. Later that day the camp was in chaos, as civilian police visited with the injured man to voice a complaint.

I saw the poor fellow and he was in a right state with swollen lips, stitches in his nose and puffed-up eyes. He was of slight build and looked a slip of a boy in comparison to the thug who had attacked him. It was only when the fragile little man talked that I detected some front teeth missing. To my delight, two MPs arrested Bullyboy and marched him off to the guardroom. He was officially charged and a hearing was set up for two days hence, pending a court martial.

'Good,' I thought. 'He's got his just desserts.' I couldn't have been more wrong.

Next morning an infantry sergeant, accompanied by the sergeant major, came to see me in the clinical room to discuss the incident. It soon became apparent that they were definitely not men of honour.

'Right, medic,' the sergeant began. 'I believe you treated a corporal yesterday who'd busted his hand on some rocks?'

'If you mean that bastard corporal who assaulted that poor little native bloke, then yes, I did.'

'That'll do, soldier. We'll have less of that talk. Keep your lip buttoned or you'll be in serious trouble! Anyway, we're here to get certain things sorted out.'

'Right, Sarge. What can I do for you?'

'*Sarge!*' he snarled, clenching his fist. 'Who do you think you're talking to, you little runt? When you address me, soldier, my title is Sergeant and stand to attention when I'm talking to you!'

'Yes, Sergeant,' I answered, reluctantly obeying his order.

'You can take that look of your face, you blown-up medic,' said the sergeant major taking over, 'or I'll put you on a charge for insubordination.'

After dressing me down and making it plain that he was in charge, he then got down to the real issue. 'Right, we've come here to sort out these trumped-up charges against one of our corporals. I've read the medical officer's version of events, which coincides exactly with what the accused says in his statement about falling into a ditch and injuring his hand on a rock.'

He paused for a minute before continuing, 'U-um, and seeing as how you treated his injuries we're going to summon you to attend a court hearing as a witness for the defence – and we want you to say exactly what is written in the doctor's report.'

'But sir, the corporal's bound to say that, isn't he? Do you want to know what really happened?'

'Quiet, soldier!' rapped the sergeant, almost frothing at the mouth. 'I've told you once already – we'll have no more loose talk. When you go into that courtroom just repeat exactly what we tell you to say – understood?'

'Understood perfectly, Sergeant,' I replied, letting them think I would go along with their hoodwinking tactics.

'Right, Private Cowell,' growled the sergeant major as they

turned to leave. 'Report to the officers' quarters at 1000 hours tomorrow morning on the dot! And don't mention the case to anyone until after the hearing or I'll have your guts for garters! Understood?'

'Aye and up yours, you corrupt lot!' I sniggered to myself. 'I'll be there all right but you're in for a shock, maties. If you think I'm gonna lie under oath you're one off. Get me on the stand and I'm going to tell the truth and nothing else.' I was actually looking forward to the challenge, despite the fact that I would be making enemies of these so-called officers and they could make life difficult for me. I couldn't wait to see the looks on their faces once they got me in the witness box, especially Bullyboy's.

Next morning, the day of reckoning, I had to attend the hearing in my dress uniform and I couldn't find my cap badge. Pete lent me his, but by the time I got to the officers' mess I was two minutes late and all the other witnesses were present.

'Where've you been?' roared the company sergeant major. 'You should have been here at 1000 hours like everybody else.'

'Sorry sir, I...'

My pleas fell on deaf ears; this CSM had a reputation for zealousness and meticulous attention to detail, and he wasn't for letting me off. He was a real swine and seemed to extract pleasure from charging soldiers for the pettiest of offences.

'I don't want measly excuses, medic,' he screeched. 'You're on a charge! Just get in line with those other witnesses and wait your turn to be called!'

I was fuming but I didn't protest because there was no point —

he wasn't a man to be reasoned with. All day I sat around with the others, waiting to give evidence. One by one they were called into the tribunal before me, while I hung about impatiently. Then at four o'clock word came via the court clerk that the case had been adjourned until the following day. I had to attend at 1000 hours again, and this time I was there with time to spare. All other witnesses were called in, leaving me with butterflies in my stomach, as I practised what I was going to say. I was very nervous, but determined to stand my ground. Then, to my dismay, the proceedings were adjourned again. On the third day an officer informed me I would be called upon around 1100 hours.

'Thank goodness for that,' I thought. 'Let's get it over and done with. I don't fancy hanging around all day again.' I was mulling things over in my mind when all of a sudden I heard loud cheering from the courtroom.

'Ye-eah! Great stuff!' yelled Bullyboy's mates as they came out of the hearing. 'Not guilty!'

I couldn't believe my ears. Bullyboy had viciously beaten the poor bloke to within an inch of his life and the Army had allowed him to get off scot-free.

I was totally shocked and appalled by the decision and the unfairness of it all. To me this was corruption at its worst. The Army hated the stigma attached to a court martial, and after this tribunal, came out of it pure as driven snow. But to my mind the presiding officers and all concerned had a lot to answer for: Corporal Bullyboy was as guilty as sin and they knew it. They'd set a standard of bad behaviour, allowing him to carry on in his evil, cruel, shameful ways. As he came out of the courtroom, he stood arrogantly on the step in a victory pose with a sly sneer on his face, and raising his arm in the air, he clenched his fist.

'What a mockery of justice,' I thought. 'It's unbelievable that he's gotten away with it.' I was fuming, but felt helpless as I knew he couldn't be tried again for the same offence. As he passed by me, he nodded and smiled but his smile was like a shadow under a stone, displaying the true character of the man... or should I say the beast. The calibre of the man was that of a snake.

At the time I didn't fully understand all the workings of the law, but with a bit more knowledge I would have reported it to the civil police and maybe the poor bloke could have taken out a civil action against the brute.

The trial was over but I still hadn't been excused. With the result going in the Army's favour, I thought that the sergeant major might relent and let me off for my little misdemeanour of being two minutes late, but there was no chance. I tried protesting but to no avail. He relished the power he held over me and seemed to derive pleasure from it; he ordered me to attention and then marched me in front of the commanding officer.

I mentioned my cap badge, as I couldn't come up with anything else, but it was fruitless. The CO, just like the CSO, was unforgiving. After hearing my plea he furrowed his brows and gave me a sardonic smile. He kept me in suspense, peering at me in silence as if daring me to intervene while he deliberated my case. I was too canny for that, having been warned by Spud Murphy.

'When you go in front of the CO, John,' he'd said, 'let him rant on and don't interrupt until he's considered what he's going to do with you; it gives him a feeling of power. Act subservient and you may get off with a caution.'

I took Spud's advice but it didn't do me any good. The CO finally came to his conclusion and gave me seven days' jankers. I couldn't believe it; it seemed so unjust and all because of a bombastic bullyboy. I resented the fact that the hooligan had been cleared and felt I was being punished indirectly because of his crime. I'd heeded Spud's advice but it hadn't done me any good; now I was determined to speak out.

'I'm not taking this lying down,' I thought. 'Even if they can't try Bullyboy again I'm gonna say my piece. So I protested, but as soon as I mentioned the incident I was shot down in flames.

'That will do, soldier! That case is done and dusted,' rapped the CO. 'I don't want another word mentioned on the subject or I'll sentence you to seven days in the cells without pay. Do you understand?'

'Perfectly, sir,' I replied with an insolent look on my face.

'Take that look off your face, soldier, or I'll have you for insubordination.'

'With all due respect, sir, I am not being insubordinate. The look on my face is borne of frustration because I feel that my hands are tied.' I certainly didn't want throwing in the brig with loss of pay but I couldn't stop myself from adding, 'I may not be allowed to talk about this injustice in Army circles but I feel it is my duty to report it to the local police.'

If looks could kill I would have dropped dead on the spot. His piercing eyes fixed onto mine and I could feel my spirit flagging. The CO made it quite plain what he thought about my remark. 'Just remember one thing, Private Cowell. You're confined to the camp for seven days and if it comes to my notice that you've put one foot outside the camp gates you'll be in serious trouble. Do you understand what I'm saying?'

'Yes, sir!'

He pondered for a while further, stroking his chin, and then dismissed me. 'Right, soldier. You can go now, but take heed of what I said.'

As I left the room it was obvious that the CO wasn't very happy with me and I had a feeling that I hadn't heard the last of it. It didn't take very long for my premonition to come true... four days to be exact.

Mark Radiven and I received orders that we were being transferred to Bamenda, 150 miles further north, into mountainous terrain.

'It must be a coincidence,' I thought. 'They wouldn't go out of their way so much... surely not?' Coincidence or not, I had to pack my kitbag and on the last day of my jankers I was heading for my second camp, way up in the mountains.

CHAPTER SIX

BAMENDA AND OUTPOSTS

A fter bidding farewell to my friends, including the natives, I climbed into a Landrover alongside Mark Radiven and we headed for our new camp. As we travelled through dense bush country along makeshift roads, I found it really daunting. We'd over 150 miles to go and I felt every bump and rut. Besides being muddy there were potholes everywhere and steep cliff drops to one side of the track. Paddy, an Irishman in the Service Corps, was driving us to Bamenda and had to focus hard on the road; otherwise we could have had a catastrophe. He had a great sense of humour as I found out when I expressed my concern.

'Bloody hell, Paddy! I wouldn't like to drive on these roads.'

'Just shut your eyes like I do,' he laughed.

To make matters worse, every now and then large juggernauts, transporting gigantic logs, would come tearing towards us at great speed without giving way an inch. After travelling for hours on end along dense jungle roads we finally came to open country and after about a mile started to climb steadily up a steep escarpment, which gave way to panoramic views over the surrounding territory. This particular region was known as the Savannah Uplands and Bamenda was situated way up the mountain, giving it a great vantage point.

In comparison to the thick jungle surrounding Kumba, this region was hilly with deep valleys and gorges covered in bamboo thickets, making it ideal for guerillas. For years, the outlaws had wreaked havoc throughout the country and despite many bombing raids, the French couldn't control their activities. It was nigh on impossible to track them down as the rebels, having lived there all their lives, knew every nook and cranny of the area. However, after the arrival of the British battalion, things took a different turn. The King's Own Borderers, highly trained in jungle warfare and close combat, were led by highly experienced veterans from the Second World War, who were used to patrolling all types of rugged terrain. Constant patrols and routine roadblocks became normal routine with only a few incidents.

When I reached the Bamenda camp I immediately noticed a difference. The air was fresher and smelled cleaner, making it more pleasant and much easier to breathe. Due to the fresher climate I often got the impression that I was back in England on a hot summer's day, but one thing that brought me back to reality was the presence of snakes. I only ever saw one but I was well aware that there were plenty around because there were always lots of skins lying around which the reptiles had shed.

The monsoon season had finished and the hot sun parched the mud so much that it gave off a red dust, covering all the vehicles and equipment. Troops returning to camp after being out on patrol looked like Red Indians.

Unlike Kumba, all billets were tents set up on grass within the confines of a disused racetrack. The cookhouse stood near the outer fringe of the camp and resembled a circus big top. Mark and I were the only medics among 40 men, as the remaining nursing orderlies were out on patrol, supporting other troops. We both slept in a tent that housed eight men, among them other attachments. One of these happened to be Neville Atkinson, my old school friend, who I hadn't seen since leaving the *Devonshire*.

I knew from back on the ship that Neville was in the Signal Corps but what I didn't know was that he was the camp's disc jockey. I discovered this on my way to breakfast on Sunday morning when I heard his voice over the Tannoy. I couldn't believe my ears when I heard him congratulating one of the troops on his birthday and, especially for the lad, he played a record by Neil Sedaka, 'Calendar Girl'. Neville must have been a keen fan of Neil Sedaka, as the next two songs he played were 'Oh Carol' and 'Little Devil'. I had a good laugh about it with him when I next saw him.

'Bloomin' 'eck, Nev,' I joked. 'You must be the first ever DJ in the Cameroons.'

'Aye, you never know, John,' he laughed. 'I might get discovered out here and become a millionaire.'

185

It was good to have Neville around, someone from my own town. I felt I was going to settle down more quickly now into my new surroundings.

Later that Sunday I made my way to the local Mankon Church, which was situated in the midst of some shanty-type huts. Like Kumba, it was served by missionaries, so I took my Roman Catholic Missal with me and asked them to sign it for me. Just as in Kumba, the priest stamped it with the church's official mark.

The hospital was very small in comparison with Kumba. In fact it was more like a treatment room and Mark and I were the only two medics in attendance. Mark had worked as a clerk so he did all the paperwork, while I did most of the nursing duties. This worked out fine for both of us. I treated the men for minor ailments and lacerations, but if a soldier took ill, he was usually confined to bed in his tent and I would pay regular visits to keep an eye on him and to make sure he got his meals. Confinement to his tent had an advantage over being in hospital, as lads around the camp would help out and encourage the lad, and troops returning from patrol would drop in to cheer the patient up.

I'd treated various conditions in Kumba, but in Bamenda I came across different ailments. No one suffered from the dreaded fungal rash but quite a few endured dreadful earache. My heart used to go out to some of the lads because the pain was so severe and constant that they felt like banging their heads against a wall. I felt a bit helpless, because all I could do was give them prescribed analgesics, but nothing seemed to ease the pain.

Eventually they would have to be transferred to Buea, and sometimes from there to the civilian hospital in Tiko. It must have been something to do with the altitude in Bamenda that affected their ears; it seemed to settle once they reached the main camp. One lad got inflammation and swelling of the lower legs, especially his ankles, and it looked like elephantitis with blisters. We were quite alarmed, as it also resembled leprosy. Another soldier had a seriously infected belly button with lots of pus oozing from it, which had been caused by an insect bite or some kind of bug. In both cases all I could do, besides giving painkillers, was to clean the wounds every day and apply dressings. There was no sign of improvement in either patient, and as they were both in obvious distress, they were transferred to Mamfe, an Air Force base with better facilities, and from there to Buea.

Once the patients left Bamenda, I didn't usually see them again, but rumour had it that they weren't treated very well at Mamfe. The Air Force boys had a reputation among the troops for looking down on Army personnel and thought we were the scum of the earth. I could never understand the logic in this because when any of the air corps visited our campsite they were always treated well.

Just as at my first camp, the soldiers employed natives to do their chores for a minimal fee. But unlike Kumba, where we had hut boys, the attendant for our tent was a young native girl called Lucy. She was very good, and like Pius Tashi, did our washing, cleaned our boots and generally kept the place neat and tidy.

I got on well with Lucy and we became very good friends. I liked her and she made it clear that she liked me. One day while hanging out clothes on a washing line she approached me and put her arms around my neck saying, 'You marry me, Mr John, I go back to England with you... I promise I make you good wife.'

'I like you too, Lucy, but it wouldn't work. England is so different to out here in Africa – you wouldn't be happy.'

She just smiled. 'I be happy anywhere in world with you, Mr John.'

I felt a bit awkward, as I didn't want to hurt her feelings. 'You may think that now, Lucy, but a few years from now things will look different. You will find a nice man out here and will have many children – you'll see.'

'All right, Mister John,' she laughed, showing her pearly white teeth, 'but I always keep you in my prayers and my heart.'

'And I'll always keep you in mine,' I replied, very touched by her manner.

The strong affinity between us was to last throughout my time in Bamenda.

Bamenda had a small market place, but it was about three quarters of a mile from camp, at the lower end of a steep mountain road. Still, I enjoyed the trek, especially now it was the dry season. It was a quaint little bazaar, which sold trinkets and other things, but mainly dealt in clothes. The items were very cheap and skilled tailors could make suits or anything else to order.

One day while I was rummaging through some wares Mark

called me over. 'Hey John, have you seen this material? It'd make a cracking shirt. It's got all the colours of the rainbow in it.'

'Bloomin' 'eck, you're right,' I said. 'I'd love one made out of that.'

'I make you shirt, soldier,' said the stallholder, waving a tape measure and keen to make a sale.

'Oh yeah, how much?'

'Only eight shillings... it very good quality.'

'No, thank you, I like it but not that much,' I answered, going into haggling mode.

'But please, it very good price and I take plenty much trouble to make so it fit perfect.'

'I'll give you four shillings... not a penny more.'

'No, no, I no can do... I have plenty big family to feed. The best I can do be seven shillings.'

'Oh yeah? I've heard that one before.'

'But I no speak with you before, sir... I no understand.'

'It's all right, it's just an expression. I'll tell you what – I'll give you six shillings, and that's it.'

'Right, you give me six shillings now... I make you shirt.'

'Whoa, hang on a minute! I'll give you two shillings now and another four shillings when the shirt is ready.'

He shook his head a little then agreed to the deal. 'Righto sir, I measure you now... you come next week and shirt be ready.'

So the deal was struck, but on the way back to camp Mark was more than a little suspicious. 'That might be the last you see of that two bob, John. You're more trusting than me.'

'You might be right, Mark, but somehow I don't think so. Anyway, wait and see.'

My gut feeling about the gentleman was right. When I went back the following week my shirt was hung on a hanger waiting to be collected. The man called me over as soon as he saw me. 'You try on shirt, soldier man… I think you like.'

I didn't just like it – I loved it. It fitted like a glove. I felt like I was in Hawaii. I wore it that night and strutted about the NAAFI like a peacock. I liked it so much that I ordered a couple more to take home as presents for my brothers.

This got me to thinking that I should also get something for my sisters. I glanced at another stall and saw an array of underslips and bodices with flower-like buttons down the front. It put me in mind of a small milliner's shop back home, which stood facing the entrance to the Market Hall. My twin sister Mary used to frequent the shop, especially on Saturdays, as did other young girls. There were some nice oddments on this stall, so once more I went into haggling mode.

Over the next few weeks I bought more souvenirs for my friends back home and an extra-special one for my mum. The friendly haggling continued, and my healthy relationship with the locals continued to grow.

The routine at Bamenda was much different from that at Kumba. Although I was stationed in the main camp, I spent most of my time working in small outposts about twenty miles away, close to the French border. The three prominent outstations were at Sante

Coffee, a disused coffee plantation, Sante Customs and Pinyin. The radio operator detailed to the assignment happened to be my old chum Neville.

My first taste of this different type of patrolling was at Sante Customs, so-called because it housed the Customs and Excise building, which was guarded by Nigerian officials and French policemen. The only road through the small hamlet had to pass through a barrier, which was raised and lowered as every vehicle passed through. Every mode of transport, be it an Army truck or a civilian horse and cart, was thoroughly vetted before being allowed to pass through to the French Cameroons.

Prior to our arrival, the surrounding area had been an ideal hideaway for guerillas for years. Due to the experience of our veteran soldiers and the hard work of the troops, things were now very different. The platoon that I was attached to had set up camp amid some old farmyard buildings close to the Customs and Excise building. The tents were much smaller than the ones back in the main camp at Bamenda and accommodated just two men, but I had a special tent all to myself, which also stored all the medical supplies.

I thoroughly enjoyed working in this small field hospital because I had lots of responsibility and, in many ways, was my own boss. I was in my element and felt as though I'd slotted right into my niche. During my posting in Plymouth I'd learned to drive and now my driving licence held me in good stead. At this small outpost I had a vehicle at my disposal, a covered Jeep which had been adapted for use as a miniature ambulance. It was fitted out with a canvas bed, splints and small units, containing First Aid supplies and other equipment.

Another tent had been erected with limited medical supplies, specially set up so soldiers could attend sick parade. There was no doctor around, so I was totally accountable for the health and safety of this small platoon of soldiers. It worked on the principle that I assessed soldiers' complaints and if I thought it necessary, I could excuse them from certain duties. If a soldier became seriously ill I got in touch, via Neville, with the main camp back in Bamenda. If necessary, I transported the patient back to the main hospital to be seen by the medical officer.

Every morning during inspection parade, I routinely gave each soldier a Paludrin tablet and then attended to sick parade. On one occasion a soldier named Dave came to the tent.

'Yes, Dave,' I said. 'What can I do for you?'

'Well, I'm supposed to go out on a route march today with Sergeant Jones' mob and my feet are bloomin' killing me.'

'Right then, take your boots off and let's have a look.' After assessing him I said, 'I can see what your trouble is – you've got some blisters forming just near your big toes.'

'What does that mean then?'

'It means you won't have to go on the route march 'cos I'm excusing you from wearing boots for a couple of days.'

'Great!' he said. 'That'll do me.'

'Here,' I said, handing him a slip of paper, 'give this sick note to your sergeant and you shouldn't have any problems.'

He didn't have any, but I did.

I was attending to another lad when the sergeant came bursting into the tent and he was fuming. 'What the bloody hell do you think you're doing, Cowell, excusing one of my squad from wearing boots?'

'His feet are badly blistered, Sarge,' I replied. 'He needs to rest them for a couple of days or they'll get a lot worse.'

'I don't bloody well care what his feet are like! He's going out with the rest of the squad and that's it!'

'But Sergeant, he can't go. If he does…'

'Shut your mouth, medic! He's going and that's bloody final!'

Not to be put off, I answered confidently, 'OK then. On your own head be it.'

'You what, soldier?' he fumed. 'Who the bloody hell do you think you are? You're not a doctor, just a bloody jumped-up medic!'

'All right, Sergeant, if that's the way you see it, *you* make him march! But I have to remind you that the medical officer has authorised me to use my own discretion in cases like this. If you still choose to send him out on a route march, I'll have to make out a report to that effect.'

'You slimy little weasel,' he scoffed, frothing at the mouth. 'Don't come the wise guy with me or you'll wish you'd never been born.'

'I'm not coming the wise guy, Sergeant. I'm just trying to do my duty like I've been trained to do.'

'Right, Private Cowell,' he stammered as he turned to leave the tent. 'You've won this round, but let's see if you win the next one, eh?'

'Oh crikey!' I thought as he stormed out. 'I hope I haven't made an enemy of the sergeant – that's all I need.'

Unfortunately I had and it didn't take long before he wreaked his revenge. I was looking at the listed orders the following day and saw that he had placed me on guard duty that night. He was out of order because all medics were exempt from doing guard and he knew it.

I approached him about it but he wouldn't listen and just started bellowing, 'Get away from me, you little creep! You'll do guard duty and like it!'

I could see he was in no mood to be reasoned with so I had no option but to carry out his will. I remember it well because it was actually my twenty-second birthday. Not to be beaten, I was determined to do something about it despite the consequences. I wasn't keen on reporting him but he'd left me with no choice.

'Sod it!' I thought. 'He's not getting away with it. If I don't mention it, he'll have me on guard duty for ever and a day.'

My superior was furious and made it clear to the sergeant that it mustn't happen again under any circumstances. The NCO didn't take kindly to being reprimanded and made things difficult for me in other areas. Thankfully, something happened to alter things and it really put all my expertise to the test.

Smithy, a regular soldier in his platoon, had a nasty accident in the foothills just outside our little station and sustained a complicated fracture of the tibia, one of the long bones in the lower half of the leg. The broken bone had pierced the skin and cut through a main artery. Within minutes, I was on the spot and the man was in a bad way. He'd lost a lot of blood and was lying on the ground in a state of shock, his breathing laboured.

'Come on, John lad,' I said to myself to calm my inward panic. 'You'll have to muster up all your experience for this one.' My mind raced back to Queen Elizabeth Barracks in Crookham, where I had undergone 16 weeks of intensive training for this kind of incident. One thing that all the tutors drummed into us during the strict regime was the importance of First Aid. They pointed out that the first person on the scene of any accident was the most vital, and made it clear that whatever was done at that point could be a lifesaver. I remembered them stressing that it's no good getting a man to hospital with a broken arm or anything else if he's died of asphyxiation or bled to death before you get him there.

'We haven't moved him, medic,' said the sergeant. 'We didn't want to make things worse.'

'Right, Sergeant, I can see your mode of thinking,' I said, after checking the bloke's airway for signs of obstruction, 'but we're going to have to get him sat up.'

'Why's that? Wouldn't it be better to leave him lying there until you've stabilised his leg? And anyway what about the wound? He's bleeding like a stuck pig!'

'I understand your concern, Sergeant, but it's imperative that I make sure his air passages are clear so he can breathe properly. I'm aware of the bleeding and I'll attend to it as soon as we have him propped up.'

'Aye righto, medic, you're in charge,' he said, assisting me to move the soldier.

'Blimey,' I thought while assessing the bleeding. He must have severed one of the offshoot blood vessels from the tibial artery. I assumed that it couldn't be the tibial artery because he would have been dead by now. Still, I knew it was serious... very serious indeed.

I applied loads of padding and pressure to the artery, but try as I might, I couldn't stop the bleeding and blood spurted everywhere. It left me with no option but to apply a tourniquet above the wound and then a large gauze dressing. After controlling the blood flow I gave the soldier an injection of painkiller to ease the hurting and help combat shock. I always carried a capsule of strong analgesia in my bag but had been given strict instructions only to use it in a dire crisis. As far as I was concerned this was one of those emergencies.

'Right, medic, can I do anything to help?' asked the sergeant apprehensively.

'Yeah, you can, Sarge. He's definitely in a state of shock – can you get some blankets to wrap around his shoulders while I put a back splint on his leg?'

'I'm with you, lad. I'll go and get some now.'

'Lad?' I thought as he raced off to a tent. He must be relenting towards me.

The back splint was shaped like a house troughing and I applied it to the back of Smithy's leg to keep it immobile and comfortable.

'There, he looks a lot better now,' said the sergeant impatiently after I'd stabilised it with crêpe bandages. 'Now, can we put him in the ambulance car and get him back to Bamenda?'

'Just bear with me a little while, please,' I replied, as I rummaged through my medical bag and took out a red indelible pen. 'I've one more thing to do and it's very important.'
I then wrote 'T 3-15pm' on the soldier's forehead.

'What the flamin' 'eck is all that scribble about?' laughed the sergeant incredulously.

'You might laugh, Sarge, but this is really important. It's to remind me that I applied the tourniquet at 3.15pm, and that I have to release it every 20 minutes to allow the blood to flow. Otherwise gangrene will set in. And it's not only to remind me – once we reach the hospital the medical officer and nursing staff will immediately be aware of the same once they see the "scribble", as you call it.'

'Good thinking, medic. Well done! Now, can we get him into the stretcher car?'

'Right, Sarge, he's ready to go now,' I said once the patient was settled down on the canvas bed in the Jeep. 'Just one favour to ask of you.'

'What's that then?'

'Could you spare one of your lads to drive us back to camp so I can tend to Smithy on the way there? I need to take care of the tourniquet. We should be there and back by tonight.'

'No problem,' he replied, quickly summoning one of his men. Within five minutes we were on our way.

At Bamenda an emergency team was awaiting our arrival and everything went fine from thereon. After filling in a report of the accident and having a bite to eat, the infantryman and I made our way back to the small outpost. I'd no sooner got into my tent than Sergeant Jones approached me.

'How's Smithy going on, medic? Did you get him to the main camp all right?'

'Yeah, Sarge. It was a bad break but he's in the best place now.'

'He is that, lad, and all credit to you. I put my hand up – I've been a bit hard on you, there'll be no more hassle from me – you can take my word on it.'

The sergeant not only honoured his word – he became quite matey towards me.

Most of the people in these uplands were farmers, who lived in small huts built of wood, clay and palm leaves. But some were herders and these hardy men used to move from place to place and build light shelters from poles and woven mats. It was intriguing to see them erect these flimsy refuges in which they passed the night. Next morning they'd be on their way, herding cattle over the rocky, dusty terrain.

Just like the main camp, the outstation employed native labour and again I made many new friends. The natives lived in outlying bushland huts scattered around our small outpost and they actually thought I was a doctor. On numerous occasions I treated these impoverished people for minor ailments and in some cases for serious injuries sustained in our employ. But I also used my nursing skills to help their families. I was committing an offence, but it seemed worth the risk, as they had nothing and might have died without my help. What was I supposed to do?

On one occasion, Kumsala, a small thin man in his early twenties, came to see me with a worried look on his face.

'Doctor John, you help me please… my wife, she is hurting.'

'And where is she now?' I asked sympathetically.

'She outside of tent, Doctor John.'

'Oh, all right. Bring her in so I can have a look at her.'

When he brought her inside I was a little taken aback, as she was only a slip of a girl and her left hand was swathed in a bloodstained rag. She looked terrified, visibly shaking as she cupped one injured hand with the other and held them both close to her chest.

'Hello there, and what's your name then?' I asked gently, trying to calm her down.

'E-e-t-la!' she sobbed, tears rolling down her cheeks.

'Eeta?' I queried.

'No, no, Doctor John,' said Kumsala. 'Her name is Estella.'

'Estella,' I smiled. 'That's a nice name. What does it mean?'

'It mean star of the sky, Doctor John,' answered Kumsala.

'That's beautiful,' I replied, looking at the young girl. 'And now my little star in the sky… can I look at your hand?'

I detected a little response but still she cowered away from me like a frightened kitten.

'Ye-es, all right, Doctor John,' she whimpered as a tear rolled down her cheek.

I carefully removed the soiled rag, but the young girl flinched as parts of it were stuck to the skin by dried blood. Eventually I exposed the wound, revealing a nasty laceration between her thumb and index finger.

'Oh dear!' I thought. 'This needs stitching and I've just promised her that I wouldn't hurt her.' My concern stemmed from the fact that I didn't have any local anaesthetic in the tent.

'It bad, Doctor John?' asked Kumsala, wistfully.

'Well, it's not serious but it definitely needs at least five stitches. It's a nasty cut, Kumsala. What happened?'

'Elephant grass, Doctor John... she cut hand on elephant grass.'

'I should have known,' I thought. The grass surrounding the outpost stood over six feet high and had a razor-sharp edge.

The young girl remained passive while I cleansed the wound but then came the hard part.

'Now listen to me, Estella,' I said soothingly. 'I know I promised I wouldn't hurt you, but now I have to do something to make you better, which will be painful. Do you understand?'

'Ye-es, Doctor John,' she whimpered. 'I understand, you kind man... I try to be brave.'

I'd done plenty of suturing before but only on soldiers, never on a young girl – I was more nervous than she was. I felt awful having to do it without anaesthetic, unlike the time when I stitched Bullyboy's hand, but he deserved the pain and for him, I hadn't felt any compassion at all. In Estella's case I felt totally different... my hands were shaking.

After spraying the wound with antiseptic lotion, I managed to insert the first stitch right into the centre and drew the skin to a close, and then made two more stitches on either side, spaced out equally. Up to this point Estella been very patient but then she became agitated and wouldn't tolerate any more. As I attempted to apply a fourth suture she kicked and screamed, and even with the help of Kumsala, I couldn't possibly complete the task. She was only dainty but she had the strength of a tiger and eventually I had to give up.

'Ah well, Estella,' I said. 'At least the skin has been pulled together, giving it a chance to regenerate. It would never have healed as it was before.'

'What is "regenerate", Doctor John?' asked Kumsala, looking worried.

'Oh, it just means that the wound will heal better,' I reassured him. 'Anyway, I'm not a doctor, Kumsala. Just call me John.'

That's what I said but it didn't make a scrap of difference. 'Yes, all right... thank you very much Doctor John!' he replied. His politeness reminded me of the similar reply that Kinton had given me back in Kumba, so perhaps I should have known better.

After dressing the wound I gave them instructions, along with some cotton pads, a crêpe bandage and some antibiotics. 'Don't forget to come back in ten days so I can remove the stitches,' I said as they left the tent. I thought I'd seen the last of Estella but to my surprise she did come back ten days later. Happily, the skin had knitted together quite well, leaving only a fine suture line.

Another time, Chimbu, a labourer, came to see me late at night and he was crying.

'Doctor John, you come to my house, please... my boy very poorly!'

I gathered the First Aid kit and followed him about 500 yards into the undergrowth, arriving at a little mud hut. The inside was typical of all the other huts I'd been in, and the little boy, about seven years old, was lying on a single bed behind a sack curtain. Straightaway I could see he had some kind of fever, as he was sweating profusely. I did my observations to find his temperature was soaring at 105. All I could do was sponge him down and tell the parents to encourage fluids.

'But he no eat or drink, Doctor John,' sobbed the mother, who was frantic with worry. 'We try all time, but he eat nothing... Please, no let our little boy die!'

'Listen to me,' I said, trying to calm her. 'The most important thing you can do for your boy at this moment is to get him to drink.'

'But he no like water, Doctor John,' she sobbed all the more.

'Just wait here,' I said, as an idea came to my head, 'I'll be back in 20 minutes.'

'Yes, Doctor John... we wait for you.'

I went straight to the stores and bought two bottles of cordial, a blackcurrant and an orange juice. 'This should do the trick,' I thought. 'It should be a luxury for the little boy.'

When I got back to the hut the mother was still very anxious. 'Doctor John, my boy, he no take water.'

'It's all right, dear – you leave it with me.'

The little boy, although drowsy, was still awake as I approached him. 'Here sonny, try this,' I said, gently dabbing his lips with gauze, which I'd soaked in orange juice. He responded by licking his lips but then after a while fell asleep. It wasn't a big response but at least it was something. Turning to the parents, I tried to put them at ease. 'That's all I can do tonight, but I want you to keep dabbing his lips like I did to keep them moist. Then mix some water with this fruit juice; I'm sure it will encourage him to drink. I'll be back tomorrow to see how he's getting on.'

I did return the next day and the one after that, and gradually the little boy's temperature began to fall. Thankfully, within a week it was almost back to normal.

'By 'eck!' I thought. 'He looks a picture of health compared to the other night.' Within a couple of days the boy was up and about again and getting into mischief.

The mother expressed her gratitude, making her feelings plain. 'Thank you so much Doctor John, thank you… my boy he be fine now, thank you!'

'Whoa!' I said, feeling embarrassed. 'There's no need to thank me – you're the ones who have done the hard work, not me.'

But the little lady wouldn't have it and continued to sing my praises. That's how it was. I continued to help the natives when in need and an affinity grew between us; they made me feel like a king.

On entering the medical tent in the morning I'd find bottles of wine or other small tokens, on which someone had scribbled, 'Thank you Doctor John'. Receiving gifts from these people, who had absolutely nothing, truly taught me the real meaning of life.

Although I wasn't a doctor, these humble people made me feel I was making a difference. It was a wonderful, uplifting experience, filling me with a feeling I'd never had before, or since.

During my time at the outposts I had to do a couple of patrols. I saw the odd propeller planes bombing various hillsides, but unlike when I was in Kumba, these were uneventful times. Nevertheless, one patrol, which I was not attached to, went out on a mission from the Sante Coffee outpost after receiving reports of guerilla activity deep inside French territory.

Awakened in the middle of the night, a squad of soldiers set off under the command of Lieutenant Olsen, a fine upstanding officer. The dispatch had been of such detail that a back-up patrol was sent along with them. One of the infantrymen in the second company, Alan Parkinson, gave a thorough report of the incident when he returned to camp after the manoeuvre.

According to his account the platoon trekked for hours through dense bush, finally coming to a ridge that overlooked a valley overgrown with tall, thick bamboos. It was amazing how the officers navigated their way through the thick jungle solely with the aid of a flimsy map and a compass. The lieutenant ordered most of the men to squat down on the spot while others surveyed the area. It soon became clear that they had stumbled upon a main guerilla camp.

'Right, men,' said the officer. 'Prepare yourselves. You know what's expected from each and every one of you. Synchronise your watches with mine... we're going in at 0500 hours.'

Most of the men felt frightened and butterflies built up in their stomachs, knowing full well that some of them might be killed in combat. Five o'clock came and into action they went, swarming down onto the camp, taking the guerillas completely by surprise. The lieutenant's offensive was a total success. It was astounding just how smoothly the manoeuvre went, with minimal casualties. Not one British soldier died, though some guerillas did.

The guerillas' camp was amazing in every respect. It was approximately 50 yards long, stepped down on different levels of the bamboo-thick hillside. The roof of the camp was constructed from corrugated tin sheets, disguised by bits of natural surrounding vegetation. The guerillas truly were experts in camouflage – the French Air Force had been bombing the wrong hillsides for months.

The design of the camp was fascinating: it was self-sufficient, housing pens of stolen livestock, cows, horses and poultry. There was a storeroom, stocked with provisions, beer and cigarettes. Another store contained an arsenal of weapons, but luckily for the British lads, they were old and from a bygone era. The infantrymen shuddered at the thought of what might have happened had the guerillas been as well armed as themselves and aware they were coming. Lieutenant Olsen did a good job and was deservedly awarded the Queen's Commendation for his action. The lads celebrated their victory over a few beers, but within days the outpost settled down into its usual routine.

I got on well with Mick the cook, and sometimes we helped each other out. He did all the cooking in an old barn constructed with oak beams supporting the roof. I'd carried some rations from the stockroom for him and he made me a mug of coffee. I was just enjoying the brew when I heard loud buzzing above and felt some sawdust touch my face. When I looked up I was horrified to see some large beetle-type creatures boring themselves into one of the large beams. They had red and yellow stripes like bees, but were twice as big.

'What the bloody hell? Let's get outa here, Mick!'

'Why? What's up?' he asked, unconcerned.

'What's up? Just look up there at those bloody things!'

'Ha ha ha!' he scoffed. 'They're just wood beetles that live in the beams – they're harmless.'

'Harmless? They don't look bloody harmless to me, the way they're boring into them beams! If they can go through solid oak that easy they must be lethal. Just look at the sawdust they're creating – they could make a right mess of us!'

Mick just cracked up laughing. 'You bloody crackpot, John! They're not boring into the beams; they live in the knotholes and that's plain, ordinary dust that they're scattering with their wings – it's not sawdust!'

I calmed down a bit but I wasn't entirely convinced. Every time I looked up they looked awesome.

When the infantry mob were out on patrol, Mick not only had to do the cooking but the washing up as well; if I wasn't too busy I would give him a hand. I didn't mind so much, but I used to finish up covered in grease and there was nowhere to wash properly. The only facility was a small bamboo table that stood outside the tent, on which we placed a bowl of cold water. We had to make do with this for both washing and shaving – until one evening I saw Mick heading somewhere with a towel over his arm.

'Where are you going, Mick?' I asked.

'I'm going for a bath. Where d'you think I'm going?'

'A bath? What d'you mean, a bath?'

'I mean what I say – a bath. Why don't you get your towel and come with me?'

'Too bloody true!' I blurted. 'I haven't had a proper wash down in ages! Just give me a minute while I nip to the tent.'

I grabbed my towel and ran after him eagerly. 'Are you sure you know where you're going, Mick?' I asked as he made his way through a patchy field.

'You'll see, John. Just follow me.'

The field was choppy and on a slight slope. As we got to the bottom corner, there it was.

'There! What did I tell you? Lovely, isn't it?'

I couldn't believe it. It was an old horse trough, full to the brim all right, but with loads of midges flying around the moss floating on the surface of the dingy water.

'U-ugh! You're not bathing in that, surely to goodness?'

'I am that! You please yourself what you do, but I'm going to have a swill down. It looks like heaven to me.'

I watched as Mick scooped away the moss and then, standing up in the trough as naked as the day he was born, he started to

207

sponge himself down. 'Br-rr! It's cold but it's mighty refreshing,' he smiled. 'Fifty times better than that bloody grease!'

'I've got to admit it looks better now you've cleaned some o' that gunge from off the top.'

'Go on, give it a try,' he said, stepping out of the trough. 'You'll feel tons better after.'

'Oh, why not? I've come this far – I might as well go the full hog,' I grinned, getting into the spirit of things. I stepped into the water but it was so cold it made all my muscles tighten up. 'Bloomin' 'eck! It's absolutely freezing!' I gasped. I was in and out in 50 seconds flat.

'There, that wasn't so bad, was it?' laughed Mick. 'I'll bet you feel better now.'

'Yeah, I've got to admit that after getting over the initial shock I feel great... cheers!'

During the rest of my time at the outpost I joined Mick every night at the horse trough and was glad of it. Like he said, it was much better than going to bed stinking of sweat and grease.

I preferred working at the outpost to the main hospital in Bamenda, and things worked out a treat because Mark, my working colleague, was more partial to the main camp. Nevertheless, I still had to do the odd duty there.

One weekend while I was there the CO put on a regimental parade and ordered every vehicle to be bulled up. It turned out to be a display of the camp's weaponry as a squad of infantrymen paraded around the camp in full battle gear behind lines of Army vehicles. One Landrover towed a rather sophisticated cannon, while another displayed the latest radio equipment. After a small mock battle, we medics put on a simple exhibition of First Aid on the so-called 'casualties'. It was all very impressive, but nothing in comparison to what the local natives put on afterwards.

Scores of ladies, dressed in the most colourful costumes, danced merrily to the sound of jungle drums and primitive flutes. Wearing traditional decorative headgear, they pranced around, displaying magnificent carvings made out of ebony, bone and ivory. These awesome ladies were then complemented by their men folk, who romped and swayed about in native attire, wielding a long spear in one hand and a large shield in the other. Every warrior was covered from head to toe in war paint, each in his own individual style. I thoroughly enjoyed the spectacle, and this was one time when the thought of an African warrior wielding a machete didn't put the wind up me.

One advantage of the main camp was that it was near a farm and the farmer rented out horses for a paltry shilling a day. I was already well used to horse riding – in my youth, my dad owned a mare named Peggy and he gave me the responsibility of attending to her needs. Besides mucking out the stable, I groomed and fed her daily, and when she needed re-shodding I would proudly ride her bareback to the blacksmith's.

So now, when I was off duty, I often went riding with one of my mates. Some of the horses were quite big but I never had any trouble controlling them. I usually started with a gentle trot,

209

gradually breaking into a canter and finishing up galloping around the disused racetrack. Some of the other lads were good riders too and we arranged races with side bets of cigarettes or cans of ale. I fared very well and my confidence grew to the point of becoming cocky – and that was my undoing.

One day, during one of our friendly bouts, a teenage group of Arabs rode up on some majestic stallions. In Northern Cameroon there was a group of Arabs belonging to the Fulani tribe. After watching the first race the youngsters broke out into laughter.

'What's so funny?' growled one of the soldiers.

'I tell you what be funny,' replied a brawny lad, who appeared to be the leader of the gang. 'You ride horses made for ladies.'

'What are you on about?' I butted in. 'These are good, strong horses.'

'Yes, they good, they strong for work on land, but no can run,' the lad replied smarmily. 'If you be fine rider, you try Arab horse... he fly like the wind.'

At this the entire band of Arabs burst out laughing and started to chant, trying to goad us into riding along with them. Needless to say their ploy worked.

'Right, you're on,' I said. 'I'm up for it.'

'Yeah me too,' said Rory, a Liverpudlian. 'Just give me a horse and I'll show you.'

That was it. Within a minute I was sitting in the saddle, clutching the reins of an Arab horse. It was only later that I found out the youngsters were from a clan called the Fulani, well known around Bamenda for their fine horsemanship.

'By 'eck, Rory,' I ventured. 'I've got to admit these are the most magnificent horses I've ever seen.'

'Aye, you're right there, John. They have a different feel about them – they're so lively.'

'Right, soldier boys,' sniggered the Arab. 'You ready? We go!'

Immediately the horses broke into a gallop, heading for the open plain.

'Oh, this isn't too bad,' I thought. 'I can cope with this.'

'Ha ha,' Rory laughed, showing he felt the same. 'This is kid's play, easy peasy… If you can ride one horse, you can ride 'em all.'

That's what we thought, but the young Arabs had other ideas. The ringleader suddenly let out a wailing sound and all the horses bolted, breaking into top speed. I enjoyed the thrill of the moment but after a few hundred yards fear started to creep in and I attempted to slow the horse down. No chance – it had a mind of its own and was completely out of my control. I started to panic, but strove to keep calm.

'Whoa boy, slow down!' I shouted, pulling tightly on the reins to no avail.

To make matters worse, one of the gang rode alongside me and with a laugh, whipped the horse's backside. It didn't seem possible but the horse moved up another gear and now its feet were barely touching the ground. All the Arabs were racing at the same breakneck speed and thoroughly enjoying themselves – they truly were fine horsemen.

'Come on, pack it in,' I pleaded to the leader. 'You've made your point – now stop the flamin' horse… please!' But my pleas were ignored and I discovered the worst was yet to come. 'Oh no!' I groaned as I saw a high stone wall looming towards me. The leading riders scoffed all the more as they floated effortlessly over the obstacle.

'Follow me, soldier man,' mocked the gang leader as he rode by. 'This is good, no?'

As the wall loomed nearer I thought of bailing off the horse but I was too scared to do that. 'Come on, John,' I encouraged myself. 'You can do this, just keep your nerve.' I mustered up every bit of experience I could to negotiate the high jump but it didn't do me any good because, despite my youthful experience with Peggy, I'd never, ever done any jumping before. By now the frisky stallion was primed up to take the wall and hell-bent on taking me with it.

'Oh well, here goes,' I gulped as its front legs took off. 'Hang on, John!' It took only a split-second but as I was airborne, time seemed to stand still. My moment of flight came to an abrupt end, however, as I was thrown from 'Pegasus' and landed on the grassy plain, taking a few tumbles. I was shaken up but luckily didn't sustain any serious injury, though I did fracture my right thumb. As I sat there nursing my bruises, Rory tapped me on the shoulder.

'Are you all right, John?'

'Not too bad considering. I think I'll suffer tomorrow, though. How about you?'

'I'm all right. I bailed off when I saw that bloody wall coming up – there was no way I was going to attempt that. I cringed when I saw you disappear over the top.'

Just then the young Arabs returned. 'Now you believe what I say?' smirked the henchman. 'Arab horse is best in whole world, no?'

'Yes, I believe you, you little creep,' replied Rory.

'Yeah, me too,' I said, holding my thumb, 'and I've got this to prove it.'

'You like I bring horses for you to ride back to camp?' laughed the young bloke.

'No, thanks,' we answered simultaneously. 'We'll skip on that one!'

As the Arabs rode off, Rory and I picked ourselves up and limped back to base. We weren't too badly shaken by our experience, but we were a lot wiser.

While at the outpost I mated out with Neville, who skillfully went about his work in the Signal Corps. It intrigued me the way he tapped out messages in Morse code on a transmitter and I thought it was marvellous how he interpreted those dots and dashes. He was the main man in charge of communications between the main camp, our base and troops out on patrol.

'Blimey, Nev,' I said, scratching my head. 'How the bloomin' 'eck you can understand that bleeping is beyond me.'

'It's easy once you get used to it, John. It's made up of dots and dashes. I just tap quickly for a dot and slightly longer for a dash.'

'Oh aye, I understand that, but it all comes through as a load of bleeps to me.'

'Yeah, it did to me at first, but after a while it clicked and now my ears are tuned into it.'

213

'It still sounds like double Dutch to me.'

He just laughed. 'Let's hope it sounds all right to them on t'other end of this wire, eh! Anyway, I'm off duty at 12 o'clock – do you fancy doing anything this afternoon?'

'I wouldn't mind going horse riding. How about you?'

'That'd be great but there's a snag – some of the lads have already booked 'em.'

'Bucked 'em, Nev? How do you mean – like in a rodeo?'

'Booked 'em, you silly sod, not bucked.'

'Yeah, all right,' I chuckled, 'I was only joking. Anyway have you got owt in mind?'

'I have actually, 'cos I heard two lads saying they'd got permission to borrow a Sterling machine gun each for a bit of target practice in the hills.'

'You're joking! I didn't think that'd be allowed.'

'No, neither did I, but there you have it. Not only were they allowed but they each got a magazine full with 20 rounds.'

'Well, if that's the case I'm all for it. We can but try.'

Sure enough, after some form-filling, the munitions officer handed over two weapons, each with a full breach. Making sure the safety catches were on, we set off with the guns slung over our shoulders. To reach the hills we had to cross a grassy plain and soon realised we were in quite an exposed position.

'I'm not going to let off any rounds yet, John,' said Neville. 'I feel quite vulnerable out here in all this open space. You never know, we might need the ammo.'

His words proved prophetic, because as we got within a

hundred yards of the foothills a large pack of baboons confronted us. The leader was a huge, fierce-looking animal, bearing its fangs and strutting about like a warrior chief protecting his tribe. In the background I could see infants clinging to the backs of their mothers' necks. I'd never been as frightened in my whole life as I was at that moment, especially when the chieftain kept bounding forward in short bursts and making threatening gestures.

The incident back in Kumba, when Pete and I got chased by a native wielding a machete, was frightening enough, but that happened so quickly we didn't have time to think about it. This time, Neville and I found ourselves in a waiting game, not knowing how the baboons would react.

'Bloody hell,' croaked Neville in a low shaky voice, betraying his fear. 'Try not to upset the leader. If he comes for us, the rest of the pack'll follow him. Come on, let's get out of here!'

'Don't worry yourself on that score – I want to get away from here as much as you do!'

To add to the nasty situation, some of the baboons were now coming round on our flanks. I felt the hair stand up on the nape of my neck and my initial impulse was to take flight. Instinct, however, told me to back off gradually.

Neville thought the same. 'Just back off slowly… don't run whatever you do, or they'll have us.'

'How about firing a shot into the air to frighten 'em off?' I replied, riveted to the spot.

'I don't know so much. It might work but then again it might trigger 'em off, what with them having babies an' all.'

So cautiously we backed off inch by inch, praying it was the right thing to do and not daring to take our eyes off the encroaching baboons – especially the menacing ringleader. Luckily for us, as we gradually edged further away from the pack, the baboons to our sides dispersed and made their way back towards the foothills. But the big one remained defiant, making a couple of extra lunges forward to demonstrate his dominance.   Grunting and growling through bared teeth, he sent off a clear message: 'Get away from here and don't come back – this is my territory!'

Even after retreating a fair distance we still didn't feel safe.

'Bloody hell, Nev!' I squirmed. 'That was too close for comfort.'

'You're not kidding – I nearly wet myself. Come on, let's get the bloody hell out of here.'

Later that night, we talked about our escapade over a few cans of beer and were further enlightened about baboons.

'I'll tell you what, lads,' said one long-serving soldier. 'I know a lot about baboons and their habitat – you don't realise just how lucky you were. They may be strange-looking creatures but they're very family orientated, and if you kick one they all limp.'

'How do you mean?' I asked.

'I'll tell you what I mean – if you'd have fired a shot, the leader would have attacked you. And even if you'd have killed him, the others would have rounded on you and torn you limb from limb.'

'What would they have done if we'd set off at a run?'

'Let's just say it's as well you didn't. Have you ever seen a dog stop in its tracks when a cat fronts up to it?'

'Yeah.'

'Well, what happens if the cat decides to bolt for it?'

'I get you – the dog runs after it.'

'That's right, and that's exactly what the baboons would have done if you'd made a run for it.'

'Bloody hell!' blurted Neville. 'There must have been somebody up there looking over us.'

'You can say that again, Nev,' I said, making the sign of the cross. 'We'll just have to put it down to experience, eh?'

'Aye, an experience I don't want to go through again. Anyway, how about getting a few beers down our necks to celebrate?'

'I'm with you there, Nev. Cheers!'

We didn't fire one round that day and after that I was never interested in borrowing any weapons.

However, I regularly had to go along with the infantry as they did official target practice and that's when I realised just how deadly accurate the SLRs were.

One day the sergeant major asked me if I wanted a go.

'Yes, please!' I replied, eagerly reaching for a rifle.

'Whoa, soldier!' he barked. 'Let's go over a few basic rules first! Have you ever fired an SLR before?'

'No, sir, but I was taught a few basic safety rules during our training at Queen Elizabeth Barracks.'

'Basic rules!' he scoffed. 'That's a damn sight different from firing one. This is an SLR, the deadliest rifle in the world. Anyway, what are the main safety rules?'

'Check that the rifle is unloaded and that the safety pin is applied.'

'Very good, but also remove the magazine, then pull back the cocking handle, working it back and forth to make sure there's no rounds left in the breech. And do you know what SLR stands for?'

'Yes, sir,' I answered, feeling smug. 'It's self-loading rifle… accurate up to 2,000 yards.'

'Yeah, and a lot further in proper hands. Anyway, don't feel so pleased with yourself just yet – let's wait until you've fired a few rounds.'

'Well,' I thought, 'I should be all right. I've won a few prizes back home on the fairground.' What a joke! It was like comparing a peashooter to a cannon.

The CSM had given me fair warning to hold the butt of the rifle tight into my shoulder before I fired, but to my cost, I didn't fully take notice of what he was saying.

'Bang!' The gun went off and the recoil had a kick like a mule, forcing the butt into my shoulder like a charging ram.

'O-oo-hh!' I cried out in pain.

'Serves you bloody well right for not taking heed!' he growled. 'Now do it again, only this time, do it right!'

'O-oh, do I have to, sir? I'd rather not.'

'Get hold o' that rifle, soldier!'

I didn't need telling twice – I could see he wasn't joking. This time I held it with all my strength, but being tensed up, it still hurt. The CSM wouldn't give up on me and insisted I fired off ten rounds. I improved somewhat but I was nowhere near the target.

By the end of the exercise my shoulder felt as though it had been through a mangle, leaving it covered in bruises.

'Bloody medics!' he rapped. 'Give it us here and I'll show you how it's done.'

He got down and fired, many rounds hitting the bull and leaving me in no doubt that he certainly was a top marksman.

During my time in Africa the indigent people never failed to impress me. I'd worked alongside them in the field hospitals, bartered with them in the market places and we'd socialised together in bars, on the football field, in the blue lagoon and on many other occasions. I thought my emotions couldn't be stirred further until one very special day over the Easter period. It was Good Friday and I had a few hours off duty during the afternoon. I was walking near the market place when I noticed a crowd gathering.

Lots of residents were laughing and chanting, and one of them greeted me. 'Hello Mr John, you come with us, we go on procession ... it be very good.'
Before I knew it I was surrounded by lots of friendly natives.

'What procession?' I asked.

'Oh, 'tis wonderful, Mr John... it is the sorrow of Christ's passion.'

'Yes, Mr John,' said another gleefully. 'It is glory of Jesus' resurrection. You are our friend and we want you come with us... you like very much.'

'I feel honoured to be your guest,' I replied, humbled. 'Just show me the way.'

I marvelled at the kindness and simplicity of these poor people as they paraded in their finery on this special day. The women stood out in their brightly coloured flowered dresses and headwear.

The road was hazardous with potholes and rocks, and when we arrived the church was already overflowing. Intermittent singing and music took place before and after the Stations of the Cross. What moved me most was that during the veneration of the cross, mothers held up their little ones to kiss the feet of Jesus. I later learnt that many of these good people had kept an overnight vigil in the church. To them the vigil was paramount to the central mystery of our salvation and many candidates were in readiness to be confirmed and baptised.

After Mass the procession got underway and again the path was treacherous. The lighting of fires, the cortège, the singing of the Exultet, the liturgy and the readings were just the prelude to something very special. Because when adults came forward for baptism and re-entered the church dressed in white garments, each one carrying a candle, the jubilation of Easter broke forth. There was singing and ululating, and people clapped to the rhythm of beating drums, while others danced alongside them.

'Come, Mr John, you dance with us... you have plenty good time!'

These friendly folk welcomed me into their midst with open arms, creating within me the most inspiring feeling. The festivities went on for three hours and the sounds of joy and good spirit, accompanied by blissful songs and Gospel music, echoed around the peaks and valleys. All this friendly merriment filled me with exhilaration.

'You like, Mr John?... It is good... no?' asked a small, fragile-looking lady.

'It is very good, I like very much... and you?'

'Oh yes... the fire is like a light in my heart and the singing gives me wings... I feel I can fly.' It wasn't just what she said, but the way she expressed herself with such simplicity.

The festivities went on and on, and before I knew it, it was time to go. As I made my way back to camp the celebrations, though no longer in full swing, were still going on. I couldn't help but think that despite the deprivation and being poor materially, these unique men and women had an undying, deep-rooted devoted faith.

'Where've you been, John?' asked one of the lads as I entered the tent. 'We've had a right shindig in the NAAFI this afternoon with some of the infantry mob. You missed a treat!'

'Oh, I don't think so,' I replied. 'I've had a really fantastic day myself. I wouldn't have missed it for the world.' I then went on to tell him about it.

'Right,' he quipped. 'There'll be no need to say your prayers tonight then! You'll have already said enough, eh?'

I knew what he meant but I just smiled inwardly. 'That's where you're wrong, my friend,' I thought. 'I now feel that I need to pray even more. Those poor souls, struggling every day to make ends meet, put me to shame.' They did, as well: they lived from hand to mouth, yet they were so giving. To me they really were living the good life that God intended.

To finish the day off I had a couple of beers in the canteen with Neville and Mark. I didn't need any rocking that night. 'U-um, what a memorable day that was!' were my last thoughts, and I fell asleep as soon as my head touched the pillow.

After the Easter period we all settled back down to the normal routine of Army life. Time passed quickly and before I knew it, I'd only one month left to serve. Consequently, it came up on orders that I was to be transferred to the main camp in Buea prior to flying home.

CHAPTER SEVEN
THE LAST SIGHTING

O nce again I found myself saying my goodbyes to special friends but on this occasion it was very sad. The natives got to know I was leaving and many came to see me off, some with tears in their eyes. They all gave me a hug of friendship and each one said something like, 'Goodbye, Mr John, I see you in Paradise... no matter how far apart, we will always be close together.' Their humility was so touching.

Finally I bade farewell to Lucy and when I saw tears in her eyes, mine filled up as well.

'I'll always keep you in my prayers, Lucy. God bless you!'

'And I keep you in mine, Mr John... Goodbye in this world, I see you in the next.'

I hugged her tightly and she responded affectionately. It was a hard thing to do, but I finally had to tear myself apart, kissing her on both cheeks.

As I turned to leave I got a bit of a surprise. Paddy, the driver who had brought me to Bamenda, was waiting for me.

'Hello, Paddy! I never expected to see you again.'

'Aye, well what it is – I get all the bad jobs.' It was plain to see he hadn't lost his dry sense of humour.

'Oh yeah. I bet it broke your heart, having to leave Buea.'

'You'll never know just how much. Anyway, how did it go in Bamenda?'

'I've enjoyed it here. It was certainly a lot different to Kumba.'

'Anywhere's better than that dingy sweaty hole.'

'Oh, I don't know so much. I've some good memories from there too.'

'You must be the only one!' he laughed. 'Anyway, let's be on our way. I have to do a detour with some supplies. We're going to stay at Mamfe tonight and then tomorrow night we're stopping at Kumba.'

'Kumba! That's great – I'll be able to see some of my old mates again.'

'Does one of them happen to be Bill Hubhoard?' asked Paddy. 'Because we're picking him up to take to him to Buea with us.'

'Yeah, Bill's a good mate of mine. He was in the same intake as me back at Crookham.'

'Oh, that'll be the reason. He'll be getting demobbed the same time as you, won't he?'

'Yeah, that's right. Anyway, did you say we're going to Mamfe? That's a bit out of our way, isn't it?'

'Aye it is, about 90 miles. But you know what the Army's like – you don't ask questions, you just follow orders.'

'It's an Air Force base, isn't it?'

'Too bloody true it is! Don't bloody mention it – I hate going there.'

'Why, what's up with Mamfe?'

'Oh, it's not so much the place as the men of the blue brigade. They're not what you'd call the friendliest bunch o' guys in the world.'

'Aye, I've heard tales about them from some of the infantry lads. Are they as unfriendly as what people say they are?'

'Well, let's just say they're toffee-nosed gits and leave it at that, eh! Get your kitbag into the Jeep – we've a long trip ahead of us and the roads are treacherous. Let's go!'

I knew Paddy was right because we were now at the beginning of the monsoon season and we'd already had a couple of heavy downpours. In fact, a few days previously I'd got caught in a cloudburst while at the market and became totally drenched. I was buying some last souvenirs when the heavens opened, with large bolts of lightning flashing across the savannah skyline. The deluge didn't last long, but it was enough to change the whole appearance of the place. As I trudged my way back up the mountain road to camp, small waterfalls cascaded down the grassy mountainside, turning the road into sludge.

Due to the road conditions it took seven hours to reach Mamfe and both Paddy and I were hungry and dirty. He was used to the routine and took us to a tent, where we were bunked up with four friendly infantrymen. After dropping off the supplies and my kitbag all I wanted to do was have a wash and brush-up.

'You'll be lucky,' laughed Paddy. 'The NAAFI and the shower rooms are out of bounds to Army personnel.'

'You're joking! Where are we supposed to wash?'

'Over yonder in that compound,' said one of the soldiers, pointing to an old semi-derelict building. 'But you won't find any showers in there – you'll be lucky if there's any hot water.'

'I don't believe this! How come we can't use the Air Force facilities?'

'Because like I said before, they're toffee-nosed gits,' said Paddy. 'I've driven to this camp umpteen times now and the Brylcreem boys have always been the same. They seem to go out of their way to make things awkward for us Army lads.'

'But surely the NAAFI and the shower rooms belong to Her Majesty's Forces, not just the RAF?'

'You may be right. All I know is there's a big notice that says "RAF Personnel Only" and they stop any Army bloke before he puts his foot on the doorstep.'

'Well, they can please themselves,' I said, throwing a towel over my shoulder, 'because I'm gonna have a shower, whether they like it or not!'

'I don't think so, John,' laughed Paddy. 'You'll see!'

'Maybe I will. There's one thing for sure – I'm gonna try.'

'Good luck to you,' he laughed as I made my way towards the RAF station.

I could hear loud voices in the NAAFI but I slipped by them

unnoticed into the shower room. It was certainly better than any of the Army camps I'd come across and there was no one around. I'd just stripped down to my underpants when a bloke walked in.

'What are you doing in here? You're an Army bloke, aren't you?' he asked pointedly.

'I'm having a shower – what does it look like? And yes, I'm a medic and proud of it.'

'But you can't use these facilities. Have you not read the notice?'

'Can't I? Just watch me,' I replied defiantly, now completely naked and stepping into the shower. He didn't answer, but just turned and walked away.

'That was easy enough,' I laughed to myself as the warm water gently eased my aching muscles. 'I don't know why Paddy doesn't use these – they're superb.' Everything seemed great, but then I heard voices and the clattering of boots on a concrete floor.

'Open up, man!' a voice roared as a wooden baton rattled against the cubicle door.

I felt rather vulnerable but tried to sound calm. 'Do you mind? I haven't finished yet.'

'Open this door now, you Army lout, or we'll break it down!' growled the voice angrily.

'All right! Steady on – I'm coming,' I replied, now feeling a bit panicky.

'What the bloody hell do you think you're playing at, you scumbag? We don't want the likes of you around our quarters!' Under normal circumstances I would have retaliated but common sense prevailed. Number one, I was stark naked and number two, there were three of them, wearing studded boots.

'Look, lads,' I said, trying to placate them. 'I've just brought a load of supplies to your camp today from Bamenda and I was absolutely knackered.' I didn't know what ranks they were, but they looked mean and menacing, and my little ploy had no effect on them.

They just stood there glaring at me for what seemed ages before one sneered, 'So you're a bloody medic, are you?'

'That's right. I...'

'Shut your bloody mouth, you maggot!' he screeched. 'Just pick up your bloody rags and get out of here now!'

'Thank goodness for that,' I thought as I attempted to put on my underpants.

'Medic!' screamed the ringleader. 'Just pick them up, I said, and get out of here! You can put them on when you get outside.'

'Right – I'm going, I'm going,' I spluttered as I gathered up my meagre belongings. I was still wet and mumbled obscenities to myself, but was I glad to get out of that place.

'Mind the midgies don't bite,' I could hear them jeering between fits of laughter as I hobbled away, struggling to put my clothes on.

'Bloomin' 'eck,' I mumbled, as I made my way back to our tent. 'Paddy was right about them bastards. He won't half take the mickey out of me when I get back.'

He did too. 'Ha, ha! Serves you bloody well right!' he laughed. 'Don't say I didn't give you fair warning.'

Later that evening, seeing as we couldn't go to the NAAFI, we both made our way to a small outpost. It was getting dark and we could see a campfire burning and hear singing. When we got there it was the four infantrymen from our tent and they invited us to join them. They were good lads and we had a good laugh together, especially when Paddy told them of my escapade. I couldn't help but compare these friendly lads to the men in blue; I knew which group of men I would rather have had on my side in a crisis.

'How come those RAF louts are allowed to get away with it?' I asked. 'Surely the NAAFI and the other facilities should be for us Army lads as well?'

'Well, what it is,' replied one of the soldiers, 'we're only passing through and there's just a few of us, whereas there's loads of them bloody mean bastards.'

'I see what you mean. I'd heard rumours of them being an unfriendly bunch but now I know about it first hand.'

'Aye by jeebers you do,' laughed Paddy. 'The whole naked truth – that's for sure!'

'That's a good one, Paddy,' laughed the infantrymen. 'We like it!' The friendly banter continued until we heard more loud shouting.

'Oh no!' said one of the soldiers. 'Corporal Bullyboy's back! That's mucked up the rest of this evening.'

'Bullyboy?' I thought. 'Surely it can't be the same Bullyboy who was at Kumba?' But sure enough, there he was. I couldn't believe it – he was standing there arrogantly shooting his mouth off and waving his arms about in the same brash manner as when he left the courtroom. He was strutting about cockily, brandishing a can of beer that was splashing all over the place.

'Bloomin' 'eck,' I thought. 'I never thought I'd see him again. Just look at the big slob, still using the same nasty tactics as when he was at Kumba. It doesn't look like there's any chance of him ever atoning for his foul deeds.'

Bullyboy's bulky frame tottered a bit, then staggered towards me. 'Get up, you little arse'ole! You're sat in my place!'

He'd only been here a few minutes and already he'd created a heavily charged atmosphere; he was a menace and I knew only too well that I had to be wary of him. I didn't want to move for the big hump of meat, but I felt really intimidated and didn't relish the position the thug had put me in. He was a big man, and at this moment he looked gigantic.

When I didn't respond to his threatening behaviour, his face contorted. 'Are you deaf or what, you little git?' he snarled. 'Move, or I'll use you as a punch bag!'

'Oh, so your hand's healed, has it?' I asked, for want of something better to say.

'My *hand*?' he queried, somewhat perplexed. 'What the bloody hell are you talking about, you little gobshite?' He approached me with clenched fist but then, luckily for me, a look of recognition came to his face. 'You're the medic who patched me up in Kumba, aren't you?'

'Yeah, that's me,' I answered uneasily.

From that moment his whole demeanour changed completely. 'Right, medic – you really put me through some pain back then and I felt like bloody throttling you, but I've got to admit that you did a belting job stitching me up – my fingers healed up a treat. Cheers!'

'If only you knew of my intentions,' I thought. 'If I'd have had my way I would have stitched you up good and proper, that's for sure.' But I kept my thoughts to myself because I knew he wouldn't have been quite so friendly towards me if he knew the truth.

He seemed to be showing a nicer side to his nature but then his true self came back to the fore, and he started to boast about his so-called victory over the little native back in Kumba and how he'd conned the Army. But his bragging didn't last long because it soon became evident that the lads were repulsed by his actions. Bullyboy actually offered to buy Paddy and me a drink, but we declined. I was relieved at the outcome because I was no match for this enormous guy, but I still felt annoyed for not having fronted up to him. Mind you, I was more disgruntled with the Army for having allowed this beast of a man to carry on in his belligerent offensive manner.

Not to be put off by this unpleasant man, Paddy and I enjoyed the rest of the evening.

'I'll tell you what, Paddy,' I said on the way back to the tent, 'this has been one day I'll remember for a while to come.'

The next morning, after a sparse breakfast, we climbed into the Landrover and headed for Kumba.

'How long will it take us to get there?' I asked.

'You're one for questions, aren't you? It'll take us as long as it takes. We've got well over 140 miles to go and it's one 'eck of a bad road.'

'Never mind, Paddy,' I laughed. 'You can always shut your eyes.'

'Ha ha, very funny. It's a good one that, because it's one o' mine.'

I had to smile. Paddy had a repartee second to none. No matter what I came out with he always had a reply.

It had rained heavily during the night and as we travelled along the treacherous muddy road, Paddy pulled up and pointed down a steep drop on the passenger side into a large gulley.

'Have a look down there, John. You can just about make out what's left of a Mammi wagon that left the road here in the last monsoon season.'

Sure enough, about a hundred feet below in the thick undergrowth I could make out an upturned vehicle with its wheels in the air.

'Bloomin' 'eck, Paddy,' I said. 'The poor bloke wouldn't have stood a chance.'

'Serves him right,' he replied unsympathetically. 'They drive like bloody maniacs and they don't seem to learn by their mistakes. I can show you plenty more wrecks along this road. It's only due to the skill of our Service Corps' drivers that none of our Army trucks have finished up down there with 'em.'

'But one of our lads *did* get killed,' I said. 'Word came through just before we left the *Devonshire* that a lad in the Royal Engineers had left the road and ended up in a ravine below.'

'Aye, you're right there. I forgot about that. But anyway, we got a right drilling when we first landed and were really put through our paces. At least our lads seemed to take heed from that, whereas the locals don't seem to learn at all.'

I had to agree with him, but I still couldn't help but feel sorry for the poor victims.

Luckily, the rain kept off, the sun shone brightly and we made steady progress. After travelling about 70 miles we stopped for a break and to cool off. As I sat by the side of a river, Paddy took a photograph of me with jungle foliage in the background, which I was to treasure over the coming years. After splashing my face in the refreshing water I climbed back into the Jeep and we continued on the final leg of our journey to Kumba.

That night I thoroughly enjoyed myself, exchanging experiences with my old mates Rob, Pete, Bill, Rodney, Maurice and Spud Murphy over a drink in the NAAFI. Apart from Bill Hubhoard, this was the final meeting with my buddies, as all the others had enlisted later than me and still had a few months to serve.

'You jammy swine, Johnny Cowell!' said a voice from behind me. 'What are you having to drink?'

'Martin Grogan,' I said without turning around. 'I'll have a Tennent.'

'You lucky sod, going back to England! I wish I was coming with you. Anyroad, don't forget to give my regards to the Burnley wallers when you get there.'

'What are you moaning about? You've only got three months to do yourself, haven't you?'

'Aye I know, but it seems like three years... I can't wait.'

It was great kipping in the medics' hut once more among my old mates.

'Do you remember when we put a lizard in Maurice's bed?' said Rob.

'Yeah, you swines, but I got you all back,' laughed Maurice.

'U-ug-gh, did you!' I shuddered at the thought of the large tarantula dropping onto my lap.

'What about New Year's Eve, John?' asked Spud Murphy. 'I'll bet you remember that!'

'*Do* I! How could I forget that civilian's wife? She was absolutely gorgeous... I could have gone AWOL for her.'

'Aye, I remember that well,' laughed Rob. 'You were well sloshed.'

'And I wasn't the only one! There were bodies flaking out all over the place. Boy, did I suffer for it next morning... I had the most ding-dong of all hangovers, I thought I was dying.'

'Anyway, John,' laughed Pete, 'how would you like a night out over the bridge on the French side? Plenty of jig-a-jig an' all that?'

'Bloomin' 'eck, what a night that was! We'd have been slaughtered if the natives had caught us, especially the one with the machete. Still, never mind, eh? We lived to tell the tale.'

'It's happen as well I didn't know about it at the time... I would have had to report it,' said Spud Murphy, trying to keep a straight face. 'Duty an' all that, you know.'

That's the way it was: fun and good humour, all taken in good spirit. I was glad to be going home, yet the moment was tinged with sadness. I'd only been out here in Africa for eight months but so many things had happened.

Next morning, Bill and I were up and ready to set off after breakfast. All our buddies waved us off with their usual wisecracks as we passed through the gates.

'Don't let the QUARANCS get you down,' they shouted.

As I left Kumba for the last time my thoughts flashed back to when I'd first set eyes on the place. Strange as it may seem, it made me feel sad.

The last trek of the journey was rather bumpy but a few hours later we were driving through the gates of the main camp in Buea on the slopes of Mount Cameroon. I was looking forward to meeting my old mates Jimmy Mitchinson and big Brian again, and as I was shown to my quarters the first person I saw was Jimmy.

'All right, Jimmy,' I said, shaking his hand. 'I hope you've been behaving yourself with them QUARANCS.'

'You must be joking,' he smirked. 'I wouldn't be seen dead with them.'

'Chance would be a fine thing!' I laughed.

'You can say that again,' interrupted big Brian as he entered the hut. 'Nice to see you again, my old mate. What's it like at Kumba?'

'It's all right if you don't mind sweltering your knackers off. Joking aside, I enjoyed it there, especially working alongside the natives. Anyway, why do you ask?'

'Because I'm going there next week to serve my last two months out here.'

'You'll be all right, Bri – honest! Once you get used to the mosquitoes, the crickets, all the creepy crawlies and the humidity, you'll be fine.'

'Thank you very much. That's all I need to hear.'

'No, kidding aside, Bri, I enjoyed it there. Anyway, how's your missus Jean going on? Are you still in love?'

That remark set Jimmy off into a fit of laughter. 'In love? He is that! Ever since we landed here he's been like a lovesick teenager, moping up and down all over the place.'

Brian took it all in good fun, pouting his bottom lip and putting on the little boy lost look. 'It's all right for you lot, but I'd only just got married when I got my call-up papers. You don't know what it's like.'

'By the way, Bri, rumour has it that you've been made up to lance corporal! Is it true?'

'That's a laugh,' chipped in Jimmy. 'He only had the tape for a week – the shortest serving lance corporal on record!'

'Ha ha, very funny,' retorted Brian.

'Come on then, fill me in,' I said. 'What happened?'

'You'll not believe it,' laughed Jimmy. 'There was a lot of graffiti on the toilet walls and the CO had them replastered and painted.'

'So, what's that got to do with Brian?'

'Well, the silly sod went and scratched a message deep into the plaster with a rusty old nail saying, "No more graffiti on this wall"!'

'Nay, Bri – you didn't, did you?' I said, trying to keep a straight face.

'All right, all right, that's enough piss-taking for one session! Any more and I'll sort you both out. Anyway, how about going to the NAAFI for a drink?'

'I can see things haven't changed much,' I laughed. 'C'mon then… let's go!'

On the way to the NAAFI, Brian and Jimmy filled me in on some of their exploits while in Buea. They were attached to C Company and lots of their patrols had been done using motorised boats to police the waters in the Delta region. Both had participated in incidents during which their platoon apprehended smugglers and guerillas.

The NAAFI in Buea was much bigger than the one in Kumba and had more amenities – it even had a stage where the entertainment committee put on cabarets. I only had a couple of cans that night, as I was rather tired after my long journey, but it was during this short spell that I was told a couple of interesting stories, both of which involved Brian.

'Have you heard about when Brian had to go to a Nigerian court because of some stolen blankets?' asked Jimmy.

'No, I haven't,' I replied, my ears pricking up. 'But I'm sure you're gonna tell me.'

'Hey, that'll do,' responded Brian. 'That's all done and dusted. I'm innocent!'

'Oh, come on, Brian! Let's hear it.'

'Aye all right, but I'm telling the tale! You know what Jimmy's like – he'll get it all mixed up. Anyway, he only knows it from a second-hand point of view.'

'Oh yeah, sure – I only went to court with you and watched the proceedings. It was a right laugh.'

'Hey, this is getting better all the time,' I said. 'C'mon, let me in on it.'

'Right,' said Brian. 'About two months ago I got a job working in the stores and a right cushy number it was. No more patrols… it was great. Well, I was working late one night and I heard some noise at the back of the hut, so I went out to investigate. As I got near the perimeter fence I saw a young bloke on the other side carrying some sheets. I went closer to have a word with him, when suddenly a Nigerian policeman came out of the bush and nabbed the fella. When he saw me he automatically thought I was in league with the chap and asked me for my details. When I refused to give them to him, he said he would report the matter to my superiors. He did too and I had to appear in front of the CO the next morning. I protested, saying I was only doing my duty because I thought something untoward was going on at the back of the stores.'

'But surely, Bri, if you'd have been involved, the stock inside the stores would have been down, wouldn't it?'

'That's what I said to the CO, so he ordered a stock check and they found that everything in the store was bob on.'

'So how come you had to go to a Nigerian court?' I asked.

'Well, the local police said it was also a civil matter and they charged me.'

'It was really funny what happened in the courtroom,' Jimmy butted in. 'I nearly split my sides laughing.'

'All right, Jimmy, I'm telling the tale,' rapped Brian. 'I don't need any help from you.'

'Come on then, get on with it,' I said.

'Well, me and the young guy were in the dock and he was the first to go into the witness box. He had to swear an oath to tell the truth, just like in England, and this is the funny part. There was a Bible, a blunderbuss and a bow and arrow, and he could choose any one to take the oath. He chose the bow and arrow! Ask Jimmy if you don't believe me.'

'It's true, John. I told you it was funny.'

'So how did you go on, Bri? Don't say you swore on the bow and arrow as well!'

'Did I 'eck as like, you silly sod! I swore on the Bible.'

'Right, so how did it finish up?'

'Well, the young bloke got found guilty and was sentenced to three months' hard labour, but they couldn't prove anything against me so I got off.'

I found the tale rather amusing as far as the blunderbuss and the bow and arrow were concerned, but I felt sad for the local lad.

'Now tell him what happened when you had a day out with Spud Murphy,' said Jimmy on a more serious note.

'Oh yeah, I forgot about that,' replied Brian. 'Well, Spud was on detachment from Kumba and one day he asked me to go into town with him. We were strolling near the market when we saw a crowd of locals around a camp fire outside a big brick bar.

'"They seem to be enjoying themselves," Spud said. "Let's go and join them." When we did, I saw they were drinking a white liquid that looked like milk. "Don't be fooled," said Spud. "That's Mimbo wine they're drinking. It's made from coconut and it's really potent. Three of those will blow your head off."

'I decided to just try a nip, but Spud handed me a big glass. It looked awful – it was thick like soup and had floaters in it – but it tasted quite good and after a couple of glasses, I felt like joining in the festivities. The locals were dancing away quietly but I was really enjoying myself – until an official came up and asked me to be more respectful, as this was a funeral.

'Well, I felt like crawling under a stone and couldn't apologise enough. The official was very understanding and said we were welcome to stay for the proceedings. So we stayed a little longer and then I needed to go to the toilet. I was told to go through the building to the back, and on the way I had to pass through a back room. I couldn't believe my eyes! There was an old lady, laid out on the floor on some kind of coconut rug, totally covered with flowers and palm leaves, with just her face showing. I could hear knocking from the outside and when I left the hut, I saw two men chipping away at a large tree trunk – it was to be her coffin. That was some experience.'

After Brian finished his tale I was again struck by the locals' beautiful culture – one that never failed to amaze me.

I'd just one week to go before being flown home and according to orders, my time was to be spent working on the hospital wards. On my first morning I was glad to find I was working alongside Brian and Jimmy.

'Now you'll find out what it's like having to work under the QUARANCS,' laughed Jimmy. 'You thought you'd got away with it, didn't you?'

'That's all right, Jimmy. I don't mind. At least I don't have to put up with them for long.'

'No, you don't, you jammy swine,' grinned Brian. 'You have all the luck.'

As it turned out the pompous ladies didn't bother me too much. With only days to go I didn't want to get on the wrong side of them, so I just got on with my work and kept my nose clean. There was just one incident when I had to bite my lip. I was changing a bandage to a patient's arm; I'd just cleaned the wound and was re-applying the bandage when she took it from me and started to apply it herself.

'This is the way we do it in this hospital, Private Cowell,' she said haughtily, 'from left to right, covering two thirds of the previous fold.'

'Oh right, thank you very much,' I replied. I nearly asked her whether she'd washed her hands first, but thought better of it.

It was during my brief stay in Buea that I had my first insight into what it would be like on a river patrol. I was off duty and I'd taken a stroll down to the river. One of the motor boats had just had a new engine installed and a team was taking it out for a test drive.

'I'd love to go with you,' I said to one of the lads. 'I've never been out on the river before.'

'You can come along if you like,' said the pilot, 'but we're going to be a while because we have to take some gear to a village a few miles down the river.'

'I'm not bothered about that,' I said excitedly. 'I'm off duty for the rest of the day – I don't care how long it takes.'

The next few hours were really enjoyable. In fact, it turned out to be one of the best times I'd ever had. As we motored down the river we passed many small fishing boats with nets cast over the sides. Luckily I had my camera with me and I took some memorable photos. The river was about 25 yards across and as we sailed past many mangroves it put me in mind of the time I spent in the swamp on patrol in the Kumba region. The contrast was unbelievable. On that occasion I was a miserable critter, whereas now I felt I was the luckiest guy in the world. The sun was beating down from a clear blue sky and here I was sunbathing under comfortable conditions.

About three miles downstream the driver pulled into a little hamlet where some fishermen were just bringing in their catch.

'It looks like they've had a fair haul today,' said the skipper.

'It does,' said his mate. 'As a rule they barely catch anything.'

As we disembarked some of the locals came out to greet us with big, beaming smiles.

'Welcome, Johnny,' said a stockily built fellow who appeared to be the tribe leader.

'Johnny?' I thought. 'Does he know me?' Slowly it dawned on me that they called everybody either Johnny or Jimmy.

As we walked into the hamlet most of the natives were sat around a camp fire, which young girls were energetically stoking with brush wood they'd carried in on their heads. Suspended over the fire was a giant wok on a grid, held up by chains hanging from a steel bar between two posts. Some women were preparing the fish on a spit, while others cooked chopped potatoes and strange-looking vegetables in the wok. The fish was then cut up into small pieces and put into the wok to make one big stew.

Elderly adults and typical pot-bellied children alike looked on in earnest, sniffing the air as the heap of chopped food sizzled away. The children's eagerness to savour the meal was obvious as they smacked their lips. This was to be their first modest meal in days and yet, hungry as they were, they waited patiently for the dinner ladies to serve out their portions. The women scooped up small portions from the wok and ladled them on to tin plates.

The wok was then taken from the fire and allowed to cool for a while on the ground. The men then sat around the now communal pan and ate from it, breaking bread and dipping it into the stew using just their fingers.

With a gesture born of natural habit, one of the ladies turned to us and invited us to eat. Once again I was taken aback by their humility and kindness. I was a stranger to them, yet they were willing to share what bit of food they had.

I didn't eat much but I found it to be a very pleasant experience as the men offered us some kind of wine in tin canisters. After our little feast I noticed some young girls carrying water using a bough from a tree, carved to fit their shoulders. The yoke was carefully slotted around their necks and a small pot suspended by string from each end. As I watched it took me back to my childhood and an amusing fable our teacher had told us during religious study. I'd always liked the tale and decided to tell it to the youngsters. They sat down in a group, all eager to listen.

'There was a little girl who lived in a small village much like this one and she had to fetch water from a river which was a long way off. Just like you she carried two small pots on the end of a yoke. Now the little girl was very fond of her two little pots and used to polish and talk to them every day. She was a happy child and her two little pots were very happy as well. All was well with the world, but sadly one day one of the pots got damaged and developed a long crack in it. Now every time she went to collect water, the girl would fill the two pots to the brim, but on returning to the village the damaged urn was almost empty. The young girl didn't mind, but the little pot did; it became a very unhappy little pot.

"What's to do, my little friend?" she asked one day. "You seem so unhappy."

"I am unhappy," replied the little pot, with tears running down the length of the crack. "I'm useless, simply useless – I can't carry water any more."

"But you're not useless," stressed the little girl, stroking its rim. "In fact you're more useful now than you've ever been."

"You're only saying that to make me feel better," whimpered the little vessel. "I'm absolutely useless; I'm nothing but a little crackpot!"'

Much to my surprise, that sparked off a fit of laughter among the children. I didn't think they would get the little joke but they certainly did and it created a happy atmosphere. That was good, but the point of the story had a far deeper meaning.

'Right, children,' I said. 'I'm glad you liked that, but let's find out what happened next.'

I then went on with the little parable:

"'You're no such thing," said the little girl reassuringly. "You are a very important water carrier and I can prove it to you."

"Oh, and how can you do that?" sniffed the little crock.

Untying the jug from the yoke, she carried it to the edge of the village.

"There," she said, looking along the path that stretched down to the river. "Do you see anything?"

The poor pot looked as hard as it could but wasn't too sure what it was looking for.

"What do you mean?" it asked. "What do you want me to see?"

"Ah," she answered, "just look to the left hand side of the path and you will see that the land is bare. That is the side on which I carried the other pot which was full of water. Now my friend, look to the left-hand side of the path."

To the vessel's surprise, the land on the other side was laden with flowers all the way to the river. "I don't understand," it said. "What's happened?"

"Well, my precious pot, that is the side on which I carried you and every day you have been leaking and watering the soil all the way from the river to the village. Because of you, all these beautiful flowers have grown and prospered; without you they would have withered and died. You have actually turned barren land into a fertile soil. I know the other pot has done a good job, but so have you, my precious little friend. Now do you see how useful you have been?"

'The little pot smiled at what it had done. From that day on it continued to water the flowers and was forever a very happy little jug.'

After the tale the children showed their appreciation by the smiles on their faces. They seemed to have enjoyed it. I know that I did when I heard it as a boy and it had stayed with me. By now it was time to set back for camp. The natives saw us to our boat and cheerfully waved us off as we headed back up the river. It had been a wonderful day and I couldn't wait to tell Brian and Jimmy of my little enterprise. It was certainly one I will never forget.

It was Jimmy's and my last night in Africa, so we decided to enjoy it and made our way to the NAAFI. As I entered I could hear lots of boisterous laughter and the star turn was none other than Clowney, who'd won the talent competition back on the *Devonshire*, and was now Corporal Clowney. He really did have a special talent and he had us in stitches with his humorous antics. His special magic wasn't just restricted to entertainment either. He had a God-given, unselfish gift for creating happiness, not just among the soldiers but the local inhabitants as well.

This came to light the following morning when I, along with my friends, was preparing to leave the camp. When I left Bamenda I got a good send-off but it was nothing like the one the locals of Buea gave to Clowney. At least a hundred natives turned out to see him off, thumping drums and playing other musical instruments. They formed two lines so he had to pass through a passageway of natives, and as he did so, ladies festooned him with garlands of flowers and threw their arms around his neck and kissed him. It touched me to see so many natives crying, their tears obviously about departure and severance; to them, Clowney was like a god. It struck me that the love and respect they had for this wonderful man was spontaneous and simply flowed from them.

I couldn't help but compare Corporal Clowney with Corporal Bullyboy. The contrast was from one extreme to the other – one was so full of love the other so full of hate. These people openly expressed their love and gratitude to Clowney, and as I looked at this special gentleman it was plain to see which of the two men was truly happier.

The hour finally arrived for us to depart. Just as the day we arrived, our form of transport was a three-ton Bedford truck, which joined others to form a convoy. As friends waved us off I looked back in nostalgia, wondering if I would ever see any of these wonderful people again. I'd only been in the Cameroons for eight months but it had certainly won me over.

As the truck drove through the camp gates I started to reminisce about meeting the Kumba natives for the first time – George, Alphonso, Dominic, Nelson, Matthias, Kinton – not forgetting our tent boy, Pius Tashi. All the fine times and the leg-pulling among my peers, the table tennis when Mark Radiven and I competed against the European businessmen, the basketball game when Martin got three days' jankers, the gymnastics, but most of all, the football match against the brave, barefooted Cameroon players.

I even pondered on the time I got seven days' jankers for a

paltry offence, whereas Corporal Bullyboy got off scot-free for a vicious attack on a poor native. My final reflection was of the blue lagoon, and I couldn't help but wonder how the little boy I had pulled out of the lake was prospering, knowing it was highly unlikely that I would ever set eyes on him again.

'Are you all right, John?' asked Jimmy Mitchinson. 'You're daydreaming again.'

'Yeah, Jim. I'm just reflecting on the good times I've had out here in Africa.'

'Oh aye? Do you fancy stopping then?'

'No, not really,' I laughed. 'I'm looking forward to going home but somehow it all seems so sad.'

'U-um, I know what you mean, but think of all the hard times as well – the torrential downpours, trudging about up to our eyeballs in mud, the night patrols, getting cut to ribbons by the elephant grass…'

'OK, Jim, you've made your point. I really do want to go home – honest!'

The trucks made their way through dense jungle country, but weren't heading for the bay where the *Devonshire* had docked, as on this occasion the Army had made arrangements to fly us home. We eventually ended up by the side of a typical jungle river, where three large barges awaited to transport us to the airport. These barges were anchored to a small wooden jetty surrounded by mangroves, and the thick undergrowth almost concealed the boats.

'Blimey, John!' said Jimmy. 'I hope there are no crocs hanging about in that water.'

'Of course there be crocodiles in mangrove,' scoffed an African guide. 'It be ideal place for them and there be plenty snakes as well.'

'Right, Jim, that answers your question,' I laughed. 'Do you feel better now?'

'Get lost! Never mind, we should be all right once we're aboard.'

As the barges sailed up river the sun came out in a vivid blue sky. A happy mood descended, giving us all a feeling of wellbeing – especially when we stripped down to our shorts to top up our tans for the last time. Further upstream, the river converged with other streams and gradually became so wide it compared to the River Nile. Every now and again we passed little hamlets and could plainly see natives on the riverbanks bathing in the cool water as naked as the day they were born – including men and ladies together.

After we'd chugged along at a slow rate of knots for a few hours, I set eyes on the most beautiful scenery I had ever seen in my life. Even as a little boy I'd always been an outdoor person and a nature lover, but this was far beyond my expectations. Beyond the lush, green jungle, standing proudly against a vivid reddening sky, was a majestic snowcapped mountain, and a glorious sunset reflected its image in the deep water. I knew at that moment I would never see anything more beautiful... no artist could have captured its splendour. I thought I was in heaven. I felt so uplifted that once again I drifted off into a nostalgic state.

This time my memories were of Bamenda. The kind, impoverished people who would give their last penny, the bartering in the market place, how they used to hail me and call me Doctor John, the warm friendships I had formed with the native workers, especially Lucy… I smiled to myself when I thought of my escapade with the Arab horses, and the scary episode my friend Neville and I had had with the baboons. Finally I thought of all the friends I had left behind. My time in the Cameroons had certainly been different and I wouldn't have missed it for the world.

'Hey, John – look at them over there,' said Jimmy, bringing me back to reality.

'What? Where?'

'Over there in them barges – they must be our replacements, just flown in from England. They're as white as ghosts.'

As I looked across the water I saw three barges loaded with troops, sailing close to our boat in the opposite direction.

'Bloomin' 'eck,' I laughed. 'Were we that white when we arrived? They're like sheets!'

All the troops on our boat started to cheer and exchange friendly greetings. 'All right, lads? Have you been bathing in Persil or what?' 'Go on, get in there and keep our end up! Show them bloody French troops what you're made of!'

'Now's your chance, John,' joked Jimmy. 'If you still want to stay… Swim across now and join that lot.'

'Ha ha, very funny. Anyway, it's too late now.'

'Do you know, we can't be all that far from landing now, 'cos it's obvious those soldiers haven't had any sun on their backs.'

Sure enough, within 20 minutes we pulled into a small docking area at the mouth of the Mungo River. The small port was in

Douala, the capital of the French Cameroons, where French army wagons were waiting to transport us to the airport. The last leg of our land journey took about 45 minutes and all the men cheered when they saw our plane, a Bristol Britannia, being refuelled on the concrete runway. I was quite excited despite feeling a little apprehensive, not ever having flown before.

The excitement reached its peak as we all converged in the airport bar for a celebratory drink. It put me in mind of when we were on the *Devonshire*, but this time there was no reason to be anxious. To add to the occasion, another medic, Johnny Church, joined us and we spent the next hour singing and rejoicing. Sadly, all good things come to an end.

'That's it,' said Jimmy, as a voice came over the loudspeaker, instructing us to go to our boarding gate. 'Come on, lads. Let's go – it's time to go home.'

It was a great feeling, especially when three gorgeous airhostesses greeted us as we boarded the plane. To top it all, these ravishing ladies waited on us hand and foot and treated us like kings. We'd just got settled when the captain announced that the flight would be in two stages and we would first be landing in Tripoli, Libya for a three-hour stop. Cheers resounded around the plane at the thought of another drinking session. It was good really, because once we reached Tripoli it gave us a little more time to say goodbye to our friends. My stomach felt a bit woozy as I experienced my first-ever landing but it settled quickly after we disembarked.

Despite the late hour it was bright, as a full moon lit up a clear night sky, illuminating another beautiful scene. We were all one big happy family as we drank, sang and laughed in a luxurious lounge overlooking the airport and beyond. As we sat there watching planes come and go, some chatted about their exploits while others broke into song as they got merrier and merrier.

'E-eh, this is grand,' said Jimmy, taking a sip of ice-cold lager. 'I could stand this forever.'

'Aye, Jim,' I responded, raising my glass. 'Cheers to the Cameroons!'

'Cheers John! I'll tell you something for nowt – I never thought that I'd be here in Tripoli... It puts me in mind of that war film that John Wayne was in.'

'Yeah, I know the one you mean, *Sands of Iwo Jima*... He played Sergeant Stryker who took the island under a barrage of Japanese fire, only to be shot in the back by a sniper.'

'Aye, that's right. It was a bloody great film. He was nominated for an Oscar, wasn't he?'

'Aye, that's right. The theme tune went, "From the halls of Montezuma to the shores of Tripoli," or something like that.'

'Well, whatever you say,' hiccuped Jimmy. 'Here's to John Wayne!'

'Cheers, Jimmy. You know something? I never thought I'd ever get the chance to go abroad either. You've got to admit, that's one good thing about Army life.'

'Aye, I suppose you're right. Anyway, here's to it,' he hiccuped again, raising his glass once more. 'Cheers!'

Shortly afterwards we boarded the plane and again the beautiful hostesses treated us like gentry. The beer and the atmosphere started to take effect and I fell asleep, to wake up only as we were landing at Stansted Airport in London. Looking out of the window, I thought I was in a different world as it was misty and raining.

'Ah well,' I said to myself, 'back to reality.'

After passing through customs we boarded a coach that took us to Euston station. It was just as well that we had said our goodbyes back in Tripoli, as once we disembarked everybody dispersed very quickly, all eager to catch their connections home. Nevertheless, Jimmy and I managed to see Johnny Church off as he caught his train to Liverpool.

'Well, I've another hour to wait before my train leaves for Wigan,' said Jimmy. 'How about you, John?'

'You're lucky. Mine doesn't leave for another three hours yet. Do you fancy going in that café over yonder for a brew?'

'Aye, why not? I could do with something for this hangover. I feel as though my head's gonna burst.'

'How about going in a bar then?' I laughed. 'The hair of the dog, as Spud Murphy used to say.'

'U-ugh, no thank you! I couldn't stomach any beer at this moment – just the thought of it makes me want to puke.'

'Righto! To the café then for a couple of strong coffees.'

We had our last laugh together over a brew and a good old English breakfast before walking to the platform and shaking hands.

'Well, John lad, that was some experience out in the Cameroons, wasn't it?'

'It certainly was… and all the better for having good mates.'

'Well, I have to go,' he said, as the platform porter started checking the carriage doors. 'I'll see you in two weeks' time back in Crookham when we get demobbed. Have a good leave.'

'Right, Jimmy, the same to you. See you later, safe journey.'

As the train pulled out of the station I stood there all alone, with just my kitbag for company. It seemed strange as a mixture of emotions – from feeling sad and nostalgic to sheer happiness – overcame me. There I was, aged just 22 and in the prime of my life, with money in my pocket, and I was going home to my beloved family and friends. I'd bought presents for my brothers and sisters and a special one for Mum, and couldn't wait to see their faces. I looked at the station clock and noted that it was approximately 30 hours since we'd left Buea.

'Ah well, John lad,' I smiled to myself, taking a deep breath. 'The weather might not be so good but count your blessings – you've got a lot going for you.'

With that in mind I threw my kitbag over my shoulder, stuck out my chest and strutted proudly to the train. As I sat watching the green fields pass by, I marvelled at the simplicity of the way the Cameroonians lived, and I felt proud to have witnessed life in its purest form. I was going home, feeling much more enriched than before my venture amid the elephant grass.

EPILOGUE

When I left Africa, the King's Own Borderers were replaced by the First Battalion of Grenadier Guards. Suspected guerillas captured by the British infantrymen during my service in the Cameroons were approximately 240, of which about a third turned out to be known rebels. After the plebiscite the southern part of the British Cameroons united with the French Cameroons to become the Cameroon Republic under the leadership of Prime Minister Ahmadou Ahidjo. At the same time, the northern Cameroons joined Nigeria.

It felt good to go home to a warm welcome from my two brothers, three sisters and Mum. One thing that took me by surprise was how much my youngest sister, Barbara, had changed. When I'd left just ten months previously she was a mere slip of a girl, but in such a short time she had blossomed into a beautiful young lady – and I told her so. During my leave I enjoyed going out to places where I could show off my tan, especially the swimming baths. I couldn't contact my mates as they were all in the Forces, so I spent most of my leisure time with my brothers.

The ten days on leave passed quickly and before I knew it I was on the train, making my way to Queen Elizabeth Barracks in Crookham, where I met up with Jimmy Mitchinson, Bill Hubhoard and Johnny Church to complete my final week before being discharged. Although we had a few nights out on the town, during the day we mainly lazed about. We all learned to be expert skivers, each of us always carrying a sheet of paper in our hands as though it was an important document. Thus, if any sergeant or any high-ranking officer saw us, it appeared as though we had an assignment. After the hectic time in the Cameroons the days at Crookham passed slowly, but eventually the day of demobilisation arrived.

We all took the same train back to London and once more said our goodbyes. But on this occasion it was different, because we all knew it was very unlikely our paths would ever cross again. Just like the previous time, Jimmy and I were the last to board our trains. That day was 13 July 1961, and I have never set eyes on him since. Jimmy was a special friend and I have been to Wigan many times on my travels but I have never been able to contact him. His address was 8 Afghan Street, Wigan, but in spite of having this information my search always came to a dead end. The first time I sought him out was approximately 21 years later but Afghan

EPILOGUE

Street had been demolished in the name of progress. Once, while on Wigan Pier, I went through the telephone directory and called up every Mitchinson in the book, but to no avail.

I have, however, kept in contact with big Brian from Leeds, and even now he still visits me frequently. Then, out of the blue, I got a phone call off Robert MacNaughton, from Halesowen, who'd obtained my name and telephone number from the Internet. Between us we arranged a reunion with Brian, and together with our wives and lady friends, we had a night out in Burnley. It was the first time we'd all been together in 43 years, and it went down a treat.

I've bumped into my Burnley mates on odd occasions and chatted about our African exploits, but when I first saw Martin after leaving Kumba he told me something that made me feel green with envy. Unlike me he, along with other troops, sailed home on the *Devonshire* and the lucky blighters got some shore leave on Gran Canarias, one of the Canary Islands.

'It was bloody great, John. You missed a treat – the young señoritas were absolutely gorgeous,' he bragged, rubbing salt in the wound.

Shortly after returning to Civvy Street I started courting Edna Simpson, whom I'd met on the night out with Martin while on embarkation leave before going to Africa. We were married exactly two years after I got demobbed, and big Bri and his wife Jean came over from Leeds to attend the wedding. Within three years my first son, John, was born and two years later Craig arrived on the scene. I'd started to work in the building trade and money was tight at first, but after some careful thought I undertook a government training course, where I worked alongside two new friends, Steve Burke and Roger Davey. On completing the curriculum I got a job as a shopfitter, working the length and breadth of England, Scotland and Wales. The hours were long, but the pay was excellent, solving any money problems. Later I started my own joinery business and worked hand in glove with Steve, taking on contract work. I did fairly well but at the age of 38 I went into the nursing profession and qualified as a State Registered Nurse, working on various departments including Accident and Emergency.

I retired at the age of 55, which gave me the opportunity to write my first book, a biography of my mother, *The Broken Biscuit*. I then went on to write my autobiography, *Cracks in the Ceiling*, and finally decided to record my personal memoirs of Army life in the Cameroons. It took me quite a while to come up with a title, but with some help from my lady friend I finally settled for *Elephant Grass*.

In May 2008 six Cameroon friends from Liverpool, Leeds, Birmingham and Burnley visited my home, where we spent a pleasant afternoon chatting about our adventure in Africa. Whenever I am feeling at a low ebb, I always think of those wonderful people in the Cameroons. It never fails to lift my spirit and I count my blessings. God bless the Cameroonians!

Incidentally, about 20 years after I was demobbed, something catastrophic happened in the Cameroons. Due to volcanic activity over millions of years, an abundance of toxic gas had built up underneath one of the large lakes and laid there dormant, trapped by thick layers of limestone. The area was not renowned for being dangerous so the authorities were unaware of the hazards lying beneath. Then sadly, one fateful night there was a small earth tremor. It was only slight on the Richter scale and didn't cause much concern, but it was enough to create a minute crack in the limestone, allowing the gas to escape. Chemical reactions took place as it seeped upward through the water and mixed with the open air. Breezes then carried the deadly poison through the atmosphere, enveloping villages for miles around. Sadly, next morning, thousands of inhabitants were found dead in their beds.

When I heard the news on television it sent a shiver down my spine. I often wonder if Lucy, Pius Tashi, the little boy I pulled out of the lake, or any of my other friends survived... I can only hope. One day, God willing, I would truly love to visit Kumba and Bamenda for old time's sake.